HOW TO
GET A
JOB IN
SPORTS

HOW TO

GET A

JOB IN

SPORTS

The Guide to Finding the Right Sports Career

JOHN TAYLOR

Bramlett

COLLIER BOOKS • MACMILLAN PUBLISHING COMPANY • NEW YORK
Maxwell Macmillan Canada • *Toronto*
Maxwell Macmillan International • *New York • Oxford • Singapore • Sydney*

Collier Books   Maxwell Macmillan Canada, Inc.
Macmillan Publishing Company   1200 Eglinton Avenue East
866 Third Avenue   Suite 200
New York, NY 10022   Don Mills, Ontario M3C 3N1

Macmillan Publishing Company is part of the Maxwell Communication
Group of Companies.

Library of Congress Cataloging-in-Publication Data

Taylor, John, date.
    How to get a job in sports: the guide to finding the right sports
career/John Taylor. — 1st Collier Books ed.
        p.   cm.
    Includes index.
    ISBN 0-02-082091-7
    1. Sports—Vocational guidance.   I. Title.
GV734.T39   1992   91-34942   CIP
796'.023—dc20

Macmillan books are available at special discounts for bulk purchases
for sales promotions, premiums, fund-raising, or educational use. For
details, contact:

Special Sales Director
Macmillan Publishing Company
866 Third Avenue
New York, NY 10022

First Collier Books Edition 1992

10 9 8 7 6 5 4 3 2 1

Printed in the United States of America

Contents

Acknowledgments

A book like this one doesn't come together without the help of a lot of different people. First, I'd like to thank the representatives of all of the teams, venues, leagues, corporations, and organizations who were willing to spend time with me, sharing their knowledge and experiences openly and honestly to insure that the information contained in this book is as accurate and up to date as possible. I would especially like to thank Pat Dawson for his help on horse racing; Frank Gallo and Dave Woodruff for their counsel on managing computers; my agent, Shari Wenk, and the man who brought us together, Steve Ross, without whom this would not have been possible; and my editor, Rick Wolff, and the people at Macmillan. I would also like to thank all of the colleagues, coworkers, and partners I have had over the past fifteen years, especially the "Rogers guys" and the people at Miller, who gave freely of their advice and encouragement from beginning to end. I'd like to thank my Mom and Dad for being there when I needed them. Finally, I'd like to thank my wife and kindred spirit, Deborah, for her constant support and never-ending faith in me and this project.

John Taylor
August 1991

INTRODUCTION

In my fifteen-plus years of working in the sports business, the questions I have answered most frequently have had nothing to do with running a sports business. Instead, they have come from people with an interest in sports, wondering what they have to do to get a job.

In the old days, which in the world of sports management means about twenty or thirty years ago, careers in sports were available only to a select group of individuals. This group included people who owned the various professional teams, racetracks, and facilities, their children, and their relatives. Also involved were a number of ex-athletes or participants in the sport who landed a front office or coaching job after their careers were completed. The remaining jobs were filled by a smattering of other people, who usually worked for extremely low pay and did everything from lining the field to handling players' mail.

With the growth of sports on television, the advent of free agency in the major sports, and the expansion of corporate sponsorships, the entire picture has changed. A baseball team that used to make enough money selling tickets to cover its payroll and turn a profit is a thing of the past. In those days, a staff of eight to ten people could handle the job. Now, major league baseball teams have staffs of over one hundred people. Players who made $12,000 a year now make $1,000,000 a year. Suddenly, the brother-in-law who never finished college isn't given the job of contract negotiation anymore. That job goes to the team's legal counsel. And the person who used to be so adept at hitting the foul shot with time running out isn't handed the job of public relations director. That job goes to a media relations specialist. Professional sports as an industry has grown too sophisticated and the money involved is too large to leave to people with no background in what they are doing.

In short, sports has changed from a hobby to a business. It has also expanded. Leagues that were limited to major cities in the

Eastern part of the country like New York and Boston have expanded, and now include dozens of cities across the continent. Eight-team leagues are now thirty-team leagues. And the number of leagues has expanded, including leagues—like the American Football League and the World Hockey Association—that were successful enough to be strong competitors and eventually were absorbed into the NFL and NHL. Add to that the growth of women's sports and the increased variety of sports offerings, and it is clear to see that the number of jobs in the field has expanded greatly.

With this expansion has come an increased level of professionalism in sports. As recently as fifteen years ago, fewer than a dozen colleges across the country offered classes and degrees in sports administration. That number is now up to over 170. This has created a pool of individuals entering the job market who have an educational background and some practical expertise in the business of sports. Now, when Madison Square Garden is looking for someone to fill a position, it can limit its search to people with advanced degrees in sports administration, just as IBM may limit a job search to individuals with MBA degrees.

The result is a combination of senior-level sports administrators wanting to pull in the most highly trained and qualified people to run their businesses and a push of people with an educational background and some experience in the field competing for jobs. This pull from the top and push from the bottom has elevated the entire sports management profession, creating many opportunities to build lasting, successful careers.

Which brings us back to the original question: what do you have to do to get a job in sports? The answers can be found in the chapters that follow, but here are some general guidelines:

1. Get the education you need. As mentioned, more and more colleges and universities around the country are offering degrees in sports management. Take advantage of them. If you have a special interest, make sure you get all of the formal training in that area available before you begin your job search.

2. Set realistic goals. If your goal is to get a job as the radio broadcaster for the New York Yankees, the chances are very good you will fail. So broaden your objectives. Determine what it is you

really like. Yes, your first choice may be to broadcast the Yankees. But what you really like is radio sports broadcasting. Given all of the different sports that are broadcast and the huge number of stations around the country doing sports, your chances have improved a thousandfold.

3. Be prepared to start at the bottom. This means working for very little money, or no money at all. This means doing things like typing envelopes, or making cold calls, or driving people to and from the airport. It means working on weekends and at night—that's when the events take place. The good thing about sports is that if you are successful in accomplishing minor tasks, you will be rewarded with more and more responsibility. Take advantage of the opportunities that present themselves.

How to Use this Book

How to Get a Job in Sports is your guide to the wide variety of sports positions and careers available. It focuses on professional, full-time career opportunities. Many jobs in sports are part-time or seasonal in nature, such as being a college referee or a stadium vendor. While these are indeed jobs in sports, we wanted to limit this book to those people who want to make sports their full-time vocation, not something with which to pick up a little extra money now and then. Also, the book concentrates on professional and college sports opportunities. While other kinds of sports jobs exist, especially coaching at the high school level and working with youth sports, these really fall more under the area of recreation management or physical education, and as such are not within the scope of this book.

How to Get a Job in Sports is organized alphabetically by job category. Each chapter contains information about a separate sports career field. Each career field is then broken up by individual job title.

For each job title, the first entry is "Education/Training." This lists the educational background required for the job, or the permits or licenses needed before applying. For many positions, this section lists not only minimum requirements, but also includes information about the kind of candidates who are getting hired. For example, if the educational requirements are listed as "College degree; MBA preferred," you know that all successful candidates for that position have a college degree, and most of them have a graduate degree in business. Many job descriptions understate educational requirements, saying a high school diploma is enough to apply. Yet when it comes time to fill the position, only college graduates are given serious consideration. This will give you an idea of what the real requirements are. That way, you can be prepared to not just be considered, but to get the job.

The second section deals with salary ranges, which have been broken up into three parts: Intro, Average, and Top level.

Intro salaries are the wages and other compensation you can expect in entry-level positions, your first job in a particular sports field. These salaries are for full-time positions, unless otherwise stated. In some cases, there aren't really any true entry-level jobs available. For example, no one fresh out of law school will get a job as legal counsel for a professional sports team. Virtually all of these jobs are taken by people with at least five to ten years of experience. So, while the job may be as the junior member of a two-person staff, it would be misleading to call that an entry-level position.

Average salary reflects the kind of income you can expect to earn if you have a solid job in that career field. This means you have been in the business a few years and are with an organization that pays about what the others pay. Of course, many things can influence the real salary you are offered. The biggest variable is where the job is located. A job that pays $25,000 in Lincoln, Nebraska, may pay $45,000 in Washington, D.C. Other factors that may affect the average salary are the size and quality of the organization, eligibility for bonus money such as from the World Series or Super Bowl, and differences in how the position is valued from one situation to another. Allowing for these kinds of differences, the average salary figure is still the best guideline for making comparisons between jobs.

Top-level salary is what the top people in the country make in that career area. In some cases it is a fairly large group, in others it is one person. The Top-level salary was included to give you some idea of what the salary limits are, and to serve as a way to compare one career choice with another. With the kind of salaries being paid to athletes today, it may be enlightening to discover just how much the people behind the scenes make. In many cases, the salaries for even the highest-ranking executives are surprisingly low.

Following the salary information is a job description. This section describes in detail what you can expect the job to be about. Of course, one particular situation may be a little different from the next. But this will give you some idea of the kinds of things that make up the job in general, and give you a feel for what your average day would be like.

Also in this section will be information on how to get this job, with some hints on things you may be able to do to prepare yourself and get the experience that will set you apart from other candidates.

After the job description is a section on where the jobs are. This refers to the geographical locations of the jobs as well as to the kinds of businesses and organizations that have these kinds of jobs available. For example, most NASCAR (National Association of Stock Car Auto Racing) auto racing jobs are in the Southeastern part of the United States. If you are interested in NASCAR racing, you should focus on that area and will probably end up living there. Another example is the career of sports photography. You can probably guess that newspapers and magazines hire photographers. But some lensmen also work for sports teams and racing facilities. By knowing where the jobs are, you will find it much easier to seek out opportunities.

The final section is "Keys to Getting the Job." This section brings you up to date on the realities of getting hired in that particular job category. For example, in some cases you cannot hope to land a particular job without at least some experience. The kind of experience you need will be listed here, as well as some suggestions about how to get it, such as doing an internship, volunteering for a non-profit organization, and so on.

It is important to note that all of the keys to getting a job in sports are obtainable with hard work. They don't require knowing someone. They don't require being in the right place at the right time. And they don't require being lucky. Many people believe these are the three ingredients to building a career in sports, and it's just not true. While nepotism is present in sports just as it is in other businesses, and good fortune can play a part in getting a job in any field, the bottom line is if you have ability, you can get a job in sports.

While we are on the subject of misconceptions, another one about careers in sports is that the job market is flooded with highly qualified people looking for sports jobs. If you have ever talked with staff members of a professional sports team about getting a job, the first thing they will tell you is how many letters and resumes they receive each week from people who want to break into the business. And it's true. I've read hundreds of them. Most of them say things like, "I really like baseball and I'd like to get a job with you. I will do anything. I've been a fan all of my life."

Teams aren't looking for more fans. They are looking for employees with very specific abilities that can be used to move a business ahead. Those people are as hard to find in the sports business as they are in banking, advertising, or any other field. If you can show a sports organization why you are the person it needs to accomplish something specific, you will soon find yourself with a job.

Summary

The reason for writing this book is to help you get a realistic picture of the sports businesses of the nineties and to help you decide where you might fit in. It's a growing, exciting field, but one that is relatively new and therefore subject to some growing pains. The information about different jobs and career pathways is current and accurate. Reading it and studying it will enable you to make better choices and put you on the road to success as you build your career in sports.

ADVERTISING

POSITION: Advertising agency

EDUCATION/TRAINING: College degree in communications, liberal arts, business.

SALARY: Intro: $15,000
Average: $60,000
Top level: $300,000

JOB DESCRIPTION: Sports jobs at advertising agencies are almost exclusively the outgrowth of having a client that (1) is a sports company, such as a professional baseball team, or (2) uses sports to market products, such as a beer or soft drink company, or (3) manufactures products used to play sports, such as an athletic shoe or tennis racket company.

While companies use their advertising agencies in a variety of ways, what they ultimately need from them are creative solutions to their business marketing needs. When those solutions involve sports, it is the agencies' job to lead the way.

The involvement in sports can take the form of using sports stars in commercials, developing campaigns and promotions with sports themes, working directly with professional teams to help them sell more tickets, or looking for and buying the best sports radio and television sponsorship packages around the country. A large, active client can spend tens and sometimes hundreds of millions of dollars in sports, all with the help of the agency.

An example of an agency that does a lot with sports is Weiden and Kennedy in Portland, Oregon. Its client, Nike, has developed an entire strategy around using athletes as spokespersons. The most successful and well known of these campaigns are the ones using Michael Jordan of the Chicago Bulls and Bo Jackson of the Chicago

White Sox. The agency works with Nike in deciding which athletes to select to do the endorsements, then develops the advertising campaign and commercials using the athletes.

The key for you is to start with an agency that has the right accounts. If its main business comes from a chain of funeral parlors, chances are slim that it will be looking for an involvement in the Super Bowl. But, if it has a tennis racket client, you will definitely have a chance of working at Wimbledon.

Given that the agency has the right client, here are the available sports positions in an advertising agency:

ACCOUNT EXECUTIVE: The liaison between the advertising agency and the client company. Responsible for managing the account day to day. Works with the client and agency personnel to develop and implement the strategic plan for the advertising. Pulls together the other departments of the agency and outside vendors as needed to accomplish the advertising goals of the client.

ART DIRECTOR: Creates the advertising. Often working in partnership with a copywriter, is responsible for coming up with the words and pictures that are used to communicate the message of the ads. Involved in all steps of the production of the ads, from selecting photographers and settings to editing the final product. The best art directors are like top athletes: they command star salaries.

COPYWRITER: The person who writes the words used in the ads. This can include radio and television scripts, copy for a print ad or outdoor billboard, or an overall advertising slogan or phrase that will be included in all advertising—such as Jay Leno's line for Doritos chips, "Crunch all you want. We'll make more." Often works in partnership with an art director, and, like an art director, often commands a star salary.

MEDIA PLANNER/BUYER: Responsible for deciding which of the thousands of magazines, television stations, newspapers, radio stations, billboards, and other communication tools should be used in the advertising campaign. Plans the "media mix," deciding how much money to put in television, how much in print, and how much in other media to communicate effectively to as many client customers as possible. Negotiates prices and contracts with media representatives. Tracks the results of the media buy. Entry-level jobs are common in this department, and are traditionally the lowest-paid positions at an advertising agency.

PRODUCTION: Once the ideas are agreed upon, people in production bring them to life. They hire and manage those necessary to film the commercials for television, to take the photographs for the print ads, and to voice the radio commercials. This raw material is worked over and edited and put into its final form, ready to be distributed, broadcast, or printed.

RESEARCH: Agency researchers are used to get the information needed to answer a variety of questions for the advertiser. Projects may include researching the acceptance of a client's new product idea, gathering opinions on the effectiveness of a television commercial, or defining who the client's customers are, and what they are like. The general idea is to get information from a small, manageable group of people and use it to project how a larger group of people will behave. For example, a study may be done to determine whether Boris Becker or Joe Montana would be better as a spokesman for a company. The outcome of the research will determine which one the company will hire.

WHERE THE JOBS ARE: New York, Chicago, Los Angeles, and San Francisco are the main centers for advertising in the U.S. Other major cities have a smaller concentration of agencies.

KEYS TO GETTING THE JOB:
• Strong educational background.
• As much practical experience as you can get. Volunteer to work on the advertising for a nonprofit group. Do free-lance writing projects for small weekly newspapers.
• Networking. Join the local advertising organizations. Read the

advertising publications. Set up informational interviews at agencies. Attend advertising social functions.

POSITION: Corporate advertising

EDUCATION/TRAINING: College degree in business, advertising, communications; MBA preferred.

SALARY: Intro: $15,000
Average: $59,000
Top level: $350,000

JOB DESCRIPTION: Haven't you ever wondered who really goes to the Super Bowl? You know that the television networks, the NFL, and the team owners get most of the tickets. Who do they invite?

Most of the time, they invite the people responsible for advertising from major corporations. It is the revenue teams generate from these executives trying to sell cars, beer, airline tickets, and gasoline that drives the NFL's financial machine. Super Bowl Sunday is a great time to grease the wheels a bit.

The use of sports as an advertising tactic means sports job opportunities within the corporate structure. Most often, however, sports advertising is only a part of the responsibility of the corporate executive. Very few companies use sports as their exclusive advertising vehicle, so the corporate advertiser tends to be more of a generalist.

Sports advertising jobs at corporations fall into two main categories: management and media.

Corporate sports advertising managers at the top level are responsible for all aspects of the advertising plan. They work with the advertising agencies to develop the commercials, to decide when and where to run them, and to track how they are performing. They are also responsible for communicating with other company departments, so that they may be able to use the advertising to their advantage with their customers and sales staff.

Much of the execution of the sports advertising plan occurs at lower levels. This may include work with the advertising agency on extending the advertising with a promotional offer, or coordinating a sales meeting around a major sporting event, or designing some point-of-sale materials with a giant football on them for use in grocery store displays.

In general, the corporate advertising manager pulls together all the resources of the company, the agency, outside vendors, and the sports team or event to accomplish company goals. The key, though, is that the corporate advertiser controls budgets. Without the approval of company management, no money can be spent by the company or the agency. That's why advertising managers get to go to the Super Bowl.

While corporate management usually encompasses all advertising functions, many companies separate media evaluation and buying into another department. The world of media changes very quickly, and it is somewhat technical. To do it right takes full-time attention, especially if regional media is involved. Companies recognize this, and that's why they devote people to media exclusively.

The corporate media executives work with their agency or directly with the athletes, teams, leagues, or events to maximize the return on their investment. In their case, that means getting commercial announcements that reach more people more often for their advertising dollar. The job consists of selecting which media outlets to use, negotiating contracts and rights fees, and expanding the media buy to include such things as free tickets for customers, luxury boxes, promotions and product sampling at the event, or appearances by athletes at selected business locations.

Media executives get some of the best fringe benefits in the sports business. They often have teams, television stations, magazines, and other companies competing for the chance to take them on all-expenses-paid trips to the Kentucky Derby, or the Rose Bowl, or the Indy 500—anything to court the favor of the people in the company who control the budget. The television networks are noted for this kind of activity. People are still talking about the great time ABC showed them at the Winter Olympics in Calgary in 1988. And the

Sports Illustrated swimsuit issue luncheon for advertisers, starring the swimsuit models themselves, is a must on many corporate advertising executives' calendars.

WHERE THE JOBS ARE: Major metropolitan areas, corporate headquarters cities, regional office cities.

KEYS TO GETTING THE JOB:
• Strong educational background; MBA preferred.
• Become an intern at the company you want to work for. Most companies large enough to have a significant sports involvement have a variety of internship opportunities available.
• Be willing to start anywhere in the company and then move to the position you want. Most companies give existing employees first crack at job openings.

AGENT

POSITION: Athlete agent, contracts

EDUCATION/TRAINING: No specific requirements, but most of the successful agents have law degrees. Some states require a license.

SALARY: Intro: $10,000 or less
Average: $50,000
Top level: $1,000,000 and up

JOB DESCRIPTION: If you believe what sports general managers say, there are more agents out there than athletes. While not entirely true, it is a field that has more than its share of practitioners and would-be practitioners.

The job of a contract sports agent is defined as helping athletes negotiate their playing contracts. It is the agent's job to work out the most favorable deal possible for the athlete, to maximize income and benefits, to help balance short- and long term rewards, and to counsel the athlete during these negotiations.

The business grew out of the realization by athletes that they knew a lot about hitting a golf ball or throwing a football but not very much about finance. They needed some help when dealing with owners or event promoters. For a lot of reasons, the results of this action have been dramatic, and today agents for key players have a great deal of influence in the world of sports.

The key to becoming a sports agent is very simple: find an athlete who trusts you enough to let you negotiate on his or her behalf. That's all it takes. And that is why there are a lot of agents out there. Sometimes the person the athlete trusts most is his father. Or a neighbor. Or a friend from college. Or the guy who bought him a brand-new car. Whatever the reason, if the athlete lets you represent him, you are an agent.

That said, there are, of course, many agents who represent a lot of athletes. Generally speaking, they are lawyers who have been trained and are experienced in such things as negotiations and labor relations. And many athletes hire management companies such as International Management Group (IMG) and ProServ to negotiate their deals. These companies generally assign one or two people to each athlete, so the actual working relationship is similar to that with independent agents. The benefits in hiring a management company often come in other areas, such as financial planning and endorsements.

A movement is at hand to register agents at the state and national level. Many states, such as California, require agents to register, pay a fee, and get a license before they are allowed to practice in that state. On the national level, some leagues will only work with those agents they have certified as genuine, reputable athlete representatives. For the most part, though, fees to get a license are so low and the criteria for certification are so loose that the same rule still applies: if you have the athlete's endorsement, you are an agent.

Most agents work on a commission basis, charging between three and five percent of the contract amount for their services. Actual fees run the gamut, from a few hundred dollars for someone doing a favor for a friend to hundreds of thousands of dollars for the biggest long-term major league contracts.

Being an athlete agent has its advantages and disadvantages. The potential for a large, steady income is real, although it is the exception rather than the rule. Athletes and athletic careers are unpredictable. Injuries, a change in a team's offensive or defensive philosophy to one that excludes his client, or a shift in careers can leave the agent without anyone to represent. The better agents represent a number of athletes, giving themselves some financial stability.

There is also the factor of prestige. Even though they represent some of the most beloved individuals in the world, professional athletes, agents in general have a bad reputation. The profession has been tainted by the actions of a few individuals engaging in such practices as paying college undergraduates money to sign early contracts with them, using unfair negotiating practices, holding athletes out of competition, and making unreasonable and sometimes outrageous demands.

The positive side is that agents get to work with some very talented, very famous people. Good ones get a lot of respect in the sports community. And the best ones make a tremendous amount of money.

An example of a typical sports-agent career is that of Leigh Steinberg. Leigh works out of Los Angeles and San Francisco, and handles professional baseball and football players. His clients include quarterbacks Warren Moon of the Houston Oilers, Troy Aikman of the Dallas Cowboys, and Jeff George of the Indianapolis Colts, and first baseman Will Clark of the San Francisco Giants.

Leigh is an attorney. He went to college at the University of California at Berkeley. It was at Berkeley that he met and became a friend of Steve Bartkowski, the Cal starting quarterback who eventually became the number one overall pick in the 1975 draft by the Atlanta Falcons. Steve wanted someone he trusted to negotiate his contract, so he asked his friend Leigh to do it. The negotiations resulted in a great contract for Bartkowski, Steinberg had a lot of fun and made some good money doing it, and a career was born.

Leigh's firm now consists of four attorneys, representing more than seventy athletes in the NFL, NBA, and Major League Baseball. Overall, the firm has negotiated contracts totaling over $100,000,000.

While there are a lot of people out there claiming to be sports agents, there is still room for people who have training in law, contracts, and especially financial planning to enter the field. The best way to break in would be to join an existing firm, as a specialist in estate planning, for example. Once there, you would learn the ropes, develop some contacts with athletes and coaches, and then be able to move into another position or develop your own clients.

WHERE THE JOBS ARE: Sports marketing agencies such as IMG and ProServ; individual law partnerships.

KEYS TO GETTING THE JOB:
• Knowing a young athlete who is about to be drafted or turn professional well enough to have him name you as his agent.
• Educational background; law degree preferred.

• Developing a network of coaches, athletic directors, athletes, parents, and friends who can help you solicit clients.

POSITION: Athlete agent, endorsements

EDUCATION/TRAINING: No specific requirements, but the most successful endorsement agents have degrees in law or in business, with an emphasis on marketing or finance.

SALARY: Intro: $18,000
Average: $50,000
Top level: $300,000

JOB DESCRIPTION: Product endorsements by athletes have been used by companies to boost sales for decades. Athletes such as Ty Cobb, Babe Ruth, and Red Grange led the way as spokesmen for products such as razor blades, tobacco, and beer.

Many companies still use athletes to endorse products. The difference today is that while fewer companies use this tactic, those that do tend to pay fees in the hundreds of thousands of dollars, and sometimes millions, to the athletes who represent them. Many an ex-jock has made more in endorsements during and after his or her career than he or she ever did competing on the professional level.

The large amount of money involved has given rise to a special kind of athlete agent, the endorsement agent. This is a person who solicits offers from companies on behalf of his client, the athlete, to endorse products.

It is much more complex than simply fielding offers and negotiating the best deal. It includes finding companies that have a marketing need that matches your client's skills. You don't want your client to have to give long speeches on television when English is his second language. It also requires developing the proper image for your client, generating enough exposure for the athlete to make him desirable to other companies, but not enough to water down his effectiveness due to overexposure.

Most of these positions are with large marketing firms such as ProServ and IMG, firms that also handle contract negotiations for athletes. These firms maintain full-time staff people who manage the appearances and endorsements of athletes and sports celebrities such as Michael Jordan, John Madden, and Arnold Palmer.

As the dollar compensation for these kinds of endorsements increases, this career field becomes more and more attractive. A word of caution, however: endorsement contracts can be even more fleeting than an athlete's career. Injury to the player, a change in advertising strategy, or a demotion from the starting lineup can spell the end of an endorsement, and an endorsement management career, overnight. On the flip side, if you manage to build a strong enough relationship between the product and the athlete (such as Miller Lite beer and Bob "I must be in the front rowwwww" Uecker), it can last, and generate revenue, for years and years.

WHERE THE JOBS ARE: Sports marketing agencies such as ProServ, IMG, and Advantage International; law partnerships across the country.

KEYS TO GETTING THE JOB:
• Knowing a young athlete who is about to be drafted or turn professional well enough to have him name you as his agent.
• Educational background; law degree especially helpful.
• Experience in marketing, financial planning. This can be obtained through internships or by volunteering to work with nonprofit organizations.

ARCHITECT

POSITION: Architect

EDUCATION/TRAINING: Bachelor's degree in architecture, design, or engineering. Completion of three-year apprenticeship and test to obtain license.

SALARY: Intro: $18,000–$25,000
Average: $50,000–$75,000
Top level: $125,000 and up

JOB DESCRIPTION: The first person a community leader, an owner, or a team's general manager will call when considering putting up a new sports facility is an architect. The start of a new building project is an electric, exciting time. What will it look like? If it is built with everything we want in it, how much will it cost? How do we make this the best facility in the country? In the end, the answers to these questions and the work of the architect will affect the lives of sports fans and entire communities for generations.

The architect works on all phases of a facility building or remodeling project, including its appearance, how it will be used, where it will be located, traffic flow management in the area, the budget for the project, the colors that are used, how it is landscaped, how many rest rooms and concession stands to include, the design of the seats, the luxury suites, the press box, the restaurants, and all of the other elements involved in today's multipurpose arenas and stadiums.

The number of stadium and arena projects under way in the United States at any one time goes in cycles. There may be no projects at all one year, but the following year six new buildings may be commissioned. Even given the cyclical nature of the business, stadiums and arenas are unusual enough and require enough unique expertise that firms that specialize in them are consistently in demand.

To an architect, building an arena is no different from building a very large warehouse. The difference lies not in the exterior structure, but in what happens inside the building. It is filled with seats. People must be able to see clearly from each and every one of those seats. Traffic must be able to flow smoothly within the building. Room must be made for concessions and bathrooms, with the proper amount for both sexes, and located in the correct part of the building. Sound must carry well in the building, with reduced echoes. In short, the architect is faced with the challenge of designing a comfortable, well-lit concert hall the size of an airplane hangar.

The sports facility architect works with a variety of engineers and specialists to produce the plans for the final product. These include experts in building materials, structural engineers, acoustical engineers, interior designers, and a host of others who help the architect meet the needs of the client.

Because of the specialized nature of the business and the great amount of cooperation needed to bring a project to conclusion, sports facility architects work in one of two ways: as part of a firm that specializes in the building of facilities, or on their own as consultants.

Many architectural firms have done work on a sports facility project at some point in their history, most often in their own city. However, a few firms have committed resources to a facilities "team" and have the experience to compete for sports projects around the country. These companies, such as Ellerbe-Becket in Los Angeles and HOK in Kansas City, are involved in almost all of the projects currently under way in the U.S., and employ hundreds of architects with specialities ranging from concession-stand arrangement to sight-line management.

For the most part, architects in these firms are expected to be able to work on all aspects of a project, from brainstorming with the owner of an NBA team about the color of the outside of the building to planning for enough bathrooms to handle a capacity crowd during the playoffs. Many of the challenges facing the architects involve ways of making the building flexible enough to handle a wide variety of events: to make it just as easy to lay down ice for a hockey game as it is to put down sawdust for the circus; to be able to convert 18,000 seats for a tennis match to 19,000 seats for a rock concert overnight; and to insure high sound quality, whether the event is professional wrestling or a piano concerto.

Another way to work in sports facility architecture is to become an independent consultant. Not every project is the Louisiana Superdome. Across the country, many small to mid-size arenas, gymnasiums, and multipurpose facilities are built every year. For the most part, these bids go to local or regional architectural firms. After winning the bid, the firm hires the specialists needed to complete the project on a contract basis. These consultants work alongside the architects from the firm, providing needed expertise in their specialty.

Examples of the most successful areas of individual consulting include acoustics, sight-line management, lighting design, interior design, seating configuration, and concession and food service design. Consultants are also used for counsel on projects that require special knowledge about tracks and surfaces, such as horse or auto racing tracks. Building a horse track requires a good deal of knowledge about soil composition, but since so few tracks are built each year, firms would rather hire a consultant than have someone on permanent staff who has an expertise in this area.

In order to build a viable consulting practice, it is essential to have built your credentials by working on a successful project, probably with one of the existing large firms that specialize in sports buildings, or to have a very narrow but specific expertise, such as the use of retractable seating or electronic scoreboard design. In areas of design and engineering that are rapidly changing or very technical, it is often more time-efficient and cheaper to hire a consultant than it would be to research the area independently.

WHERE THE JOBS ARE: Architectural firms, located throughout the country. Firms specializing in athletic facilities in Los Angeles and Kansas City.

KEYS TO GETTING THE JOB:
• Educational background in architecture.
• Experience in sports facility architecture. Get this by doing internships and apprenticeships with firms that specialize in sports facilities, or with a firm that has a current sports facility project.

ASSOCIATIONS, AMATEUR

POSITION: Management of amateur athletic association

EDUCATION/TRAINING: College degree usually required.

SALARY: Intro: $12,000
Average: $25,000
Top level: $50,000

JOB DESCRIPTION: Most of amateur athletics, including the Olympic sports, are governed and administrated by their respective amateur athletic organizations. For example, track and field is governed by The Athletic Congress (TAC), gymnastics by the U.S. Gymnastics Federation, and so on. The size and complexity of these groups vary tremendously. Most often, the size of an organization correlates with the number of participants in that sport. Groups representing track and field, swimming, and gymnastics are the largest, numbering from twenty to thirty people, while the governing bodies of sports like archery and bobsledding are much smaller.

The work these organizations do is surprisingly similar, despite the differences in the sports. The primary functions are:
1. Management of the association membership.
2. Development of opportunities for athletes and teams to compete.
3. Communications/public relations.
4. Marketing/revenue generation.
5. Event production.
6. Accounting/business management.

The jobs available in any amateur organization will be an outgrowth of these functions. For example, marketing jobs at the U.S. Gymnastics Federation include working with corporate sponsors, developing and selling gymnastics merchandise, producing and selling ads for publications, negotiating and managing broadcast rights arrangements with the television networks, and working with the event production people on things like generating revenue from signage sponsors and ticket sales.

Keep in mind that these are nonprofit organizations, relying primarily on the help of volunteers. The salary and benefits available are limited, and most of the employees perform more than one job. For a chance to get hands-on experience, however, few opportunities are better.

WHERE THE JOBS ARE: Headquarters of amateur associations, many of which are located in Colorado Springs, Colorado.

KEYS TO GETTING THE JOB:
• Thorough understanding of the sport.
• Willingness to work for small salary.
• Ability to produce results with limited financial backing.

ASSOCIATIONS, PROFESSIONAL

POSITION: Management of professional sports associations

EDUCATION/TRAINING: Bachelor's degree; master's degree for some positions.

SALARY: Intro: $15,000
Average: $50,000
Top level: $3.5 million

JOB DESCRIPTION: For the purposes of this book, professional sports associations are defined as groups that preside over sports that pay the competitors directly to compete in that sport.

Professional sports associations can be divided into two groups: those that preside over sports that pay the athletes a salary to compete, and those that preside over sports that offer prize money which the athletes compete for.

The first group includes all the mainstream team sports: the National Basketball Association, the National Football League, the National Hockey League, Major League Baseball, the Continental Basketball Association, among others.

The second group includes all the auto racing organizations, such as NASCAR, CART, the NHRA, IHRA, and IMSA; the individual professional sports such as golf (PGA, LPGA, and Seniors Tour), tennis (ATP and WTA tours), boxing (WBA, WBC, IBF), bowling (Professional Bowler's Association), and rodeo (Professional Rodeo Cowboys Association); plus the racing sports such as thoroughbred horse racing, greyhound dog racing, and harness racing.

Despite the differences between the sports, all of these associations employ people to perform more or less the same tasks. Foremost among these is to insure that the competition is fair, safe, and entertaining for the fans. All of the professional associations are in the entertainment business, and they all want to put on a good show. This area includes such things as making and enforcing rules, officiating the sports, checking eligibility of competitors, and making sure the fields and facilities at which the events take place are of consistent quality.

The second major function of sports associations is the generation of revenue. Jobs here are mainly in the area of sales and marketing. The jobs include working with broadcast rights and ticket sales, developing corporate sponsorships, merchandising programs, and sales opportunities to generate the income needed to pay the staff and participants and to turn a profit. Many associations have separate branches that are devoted entirely to this part of the business, such as NFL Properties and NBA Properties.

The third area of opportunity within a professional association is the area of information management. This is most commonly referred to as public relations. Maximizing electronic and print exposure for its product is crucial to the success and growth of any organization's sport, and it is the association that takes the lead in this area.

The fourth main division of sports association jobs falls under the category of administration. This includes things such as accounting, legal services, contract administration, and personnel matters such as retirement and benefits—in short, the management of the financial end of the business.

To get a job with a professional sports organization requires skills or experience in one of these four areas. In many cases, the leagues and sports governing bodies hire people from within the sport, say from a team or an existing tournament. Nevertheless, some jobs within a league structure call for a particular expertise. Many of the legal counsel, computer, and financial positions fall in this category. These jobs are filled from outside the sport, giving people with more diversified backgrounds a chance to get into the field.

In addition, most of the top two dozen sports organizations have at least some sort of internship programs. These are short-term, entry-level positions for students or recent graduates designed to give them a chance to get some experience at the league or association level. For example, Major League Baseball has had an extensive, successful internship program for over ten years, with many of its graduates currently in league or team positions.

The bottom line to getting a job with a professional sports organization is identifying the particular needs of the organization you are interested in and developing the expertise required to fill those needs. For example, based on their current trend if you want to get into the National Basketball Association financial office, a master's degree in accounting coupled with the ability to speak a variety of European languages would be a great position from which to start.

WHERE THE JOBS ARE: Headquarter cities, most notably New York City.

KEYS TO GETTING THE JOB:
• Serve as an intern with the organization you are interested in.
• Develop expertise in particular areas, such as computers, public relations, or marketing.
• Get experience with a member team, tournament, or event, either as a full- or part-time employee or a key "game day" volunteer.

ATTORNEY

POSITION: Association/organization in-house counsel

EDUCATION/TRAINING: Law degree; private practice experience.

SALARY: Intro: Not applicable (no junior-level positions)
Average: $100,000–$150,000
Top level: $250,000–$350,000

JOB DESCRIPTION: Most of the major organizations in sports, such as the NFL, NBA, NCAA, and Major League Baseball, have their own in-house legal staff. These positions are typically filled with top-level, experienced attorneys, who come to the associations from private practice. The responsibilities of these attorneys include contracts, licensing, infringement and enforcement, trademarks, legal administration, labor relations, grievances, eligibility and college relations, constitution and bylaw interpretation, and some broadcast law.

For the most part, these lawyers are not litigators. They very rarely stand up in court in front of a judge and argue cases. Most of the litigation work is handled by outside firms hired by the league. However, these firms are supervised by the in-house staff.

Getting a job with these organizations requires a close look at what they do, and matching that to your expertise and interests.

Large organizations like the NFL and the NCAA are engaged in a lot of labor relations work, long bouts of litigation, and extensive projects in the areas of contracts and licensing agreements. They work a great deal on interpreting the rules of the organization. Getting a job with these organizations usually requires extensive background in one of these particular areas, as well as familiarity with some members of the organization.

Smaller organizations, such as amateur athletic organizations, also have need for legal advice. These groups are more inclined to look for someone who is a bit of a generalist, who can handle a variety of legal projects as well as some other administrative functions. These positions are generally filled by people familiar to the organization. To get one of these jobs may require doing some pro bono work on a group's behalf, or consulting on a specific project or two to gain some experience with it and let its members get to know you.

WHERE THE JOBS ARE: Headquarter cities for associations, primarily New York City.

KEYS TO GETTING THE JOB:
• Build a strong record of legal achievement with clients whose problems or concerns are similar to the ones the leagues deal with regularly.
• Do something that gains a reputation among individuals who are influential with the league, such as team owners and league administrators.

POSITION: Law firm, sports law specialty

EDUCATION/TRAINING: Law degree.

SALARY: Intro: $35,000
Average: $55,000
Top level: $400,000 plus (partner)

JOB DESCRIPTION: There are law firms across the country, in every state in the union, that handle some work that could fall under the category of sports law. They negotiate contracts for athletes. They represent facilities in licensing disputes. They handle trademark problems for major events, or they help a team with a civil suit.

Most law firms do not have enough business from any one sports entity to hire significant numbers of people to work in sports exclusively. The work tends to be seasonal and project-intensive. When a major lawsuit is under way, the firm uses a lot of associates to work on it, usually under the direction of a senior partner. When the suit is over, everyone has to move on to other projects.

However, there are some firms that do have a significant volume of this kind of work. Virtually every team in every sport has a relationship with an outside firm. So do the major facilities around the country. By aligning yourself with one of these firms, you will have a great opportunity to do some work in sports. Much of this work will be very similar to that done for the majority of a firm's clients: handling tax matters, drafting contracts, doing legal administration, and, in some cases, litigating.

The benefits of seeking out and joining the right firm is that it can give you exposure to top management in sports. It can also put you in close contact with the athletes, most of whom turn to a lawyer to negotiate their playing contracts and endorsement deals. In some instances it even means working on some very high-profile cases. All of these things could eventually lead to a full-time job as a sports attorney.

Getting a job with a law firm that has sports business is no different from getting a job with any law firm. It takes a solid educational background and good recommendations. A good way to get a foot in the door is by serving as a clerk at one or more firms during breaks from law school. That way, they will get to know you and you will be in a better position to get a job once you graduate.

WHERE THE JOBS ARE: Law firms around the country that have affiliations with sports teams, venues, promoters, or events.

KEYS TO GETTING THE JOB:
- Go to work for the right firm. If you want to work with your local baseball team but a competing firm already has its business, you won't have a chance.
- Become the sports expert. Do the extra reading, the extra research. Ask to help on the sports cases, in any role. Soon you will be a valuable member of the team.

POSITION: Team counsel

EDUCATION/TRAINING: Law degree; experience in contracts and labor law.

SALARY: Intro: $30,000
Average: $100,000
Top level: $500,000

JOB DESCRIPTION: About a quarter of the teams in professional sports in the United States have attorneys on their staff. Their responsibilities are usually quite broad, including dealing with tax matters, player contracts, labor and grievance questions, and employee benefits programs; working with the league on interpretations of the constitution and bylaws; and making sure the team follows all laws and agreements on waiving, releasing, and signing players.

In almost every case, the general counsel for the team has other duties as well. These can include acting as the contact person for the facility used, managing the administrative staff, acting as the liaison with the league, and working with outside counsel on litigation matters.

To get a job with a team, most of the attorneys working today started by building a relationship with the owner of the team for a number of years. Good work on one aspect of the owner's business translated into opportunities in the owner's sports business. An example of this is the San Francisco 49ers. Team owner Eddie DeBartolo was very pleased with the work his attorney, Carmen Policy, did for the family. He was asked to help with the football business, and eventually became president of the team.

WHERE THE JOBS ARE: Major metropolitan areas.

KEYS TO GETTING THIS JOB:
• Building a professional reputation, one that gains the attention of the owner or top-level team/event management.
• Developing skills in other areas, such as management and administration, which can be better applied to the more general needs of a sports team.

AUTO RACING

POSITION: Sanctioning body management

EDUCATION/TRAINING: No specific requirements; degree in business or management preferred.

SALARY: Intro: $20,000
Average: $45,000
Top level: $350,000

JOB DESCRIPTION: Professional motor sports sanctioning bodies are many and varied, with lots of different levels of competition and different areas of the country represented. For this section, we are referring to the national or major regional organizations such as NASCAR, CART, IMSA, and the NHRA.

The organizations that govern motor sports are similar to other national sports groups, such as the National Football League and the Professional Golfers' Association. Their main purpose is to manage and promote their sport.

The nature of racing requires a number of people in technical areas. This group includes timers, racing stewards and officials, starters, scorers, and registrars. These are the people who insure that the cars and drivers are competing within the rules set down by the sanctioning body.

Another key function of the sanctioning body is the marketing and promotion of the sport. This includes developing sponsors, working with the media, and continually creating new ways for companies and fans to get involved in racing. Corporate support and sponsorship are essential to racing, due to the high cost of developing, building, and operating race cars. For example, developing and running a competitive Indy car for the entire CART circuit can cost in the millions of dollars. The marketing directors and promotions staff for the sanctioning body work to help defray those costs by getting sponsors to underwrite the entire series and giving teams an equal chance to share in those monies.

Public relations is a very important part of the equation. Media relations specialists work with print and electronic journalists from around the country to make sure fans get the latest information about their favorite team or favorite driver, updates from the latest race, and preview looks at races to come. Many people feel that the public relations specialists for racing sanctioning bodies are among the most sophisticated in sports. This is probably due to their long exposure to and experience with sponsor companies. Major marketers who use racing to enhance their brands bring the same kind of expertise to their racing properties as they do to things like television production and media placement. This rubs off on the public relations staff, and elevates the entire sport.

All of the major sanctioning bodies have staff positions that require people to travel to races around the country, following the circuit. A few groups maintain regional offices to oversee racing on a more localized level and participate in selected circuit races in their area.

One thing to keep in mind is that racing is one of those sports which takes place on weekends in the spring, summer, and early fall. In many positions, it is not uncommon to work seven, eight, or even ten or more weekends in a row. For those who love racing, and would be there anyway, it is a little slice of heaven here on earth. But being gone every weekend can put pressure on families and relationships, something that should always be considered when making career decisions.

POSITION: Equipment manufacture

EDUCATION/TRAINING: No specific requirements, but a degree in engineering preferred.

SALARY: Intro: $20,000
Average: $40,000
Top level: $250,000

JOB DESCRIPTION: Race cars are miniature engineering laboratories. They are the test vehicles for the latest developments in chassis design, engine manufacture, and braking and steering systems. Even such benefits as reduced fuel consumption, enhanced driver comfort, and more accurate and readable gauges have come from racing. A driver is only as good as his equipment, making the development and building of that equipment a key part of any racing effort.

Race cars and parts are designed and manufactured in a variety of settings, from huge corporate factories to backyard garages. Jobs in this field cover the same wide range. If you have the background, the ingenuity, and the patience to get a few more horsepower from an engine or ten more laps from a set of tires, there is a place for you in the world of racing-equipment design and manufacture.

Getting a job in this area usually requires starting at the bottom, working with a race team or a manufacturer in an entry-level capacity. A good way to start is to get a degree in automotive engineering. This is especially true for mid-size to large equipment manufacturers. But it is not an absolute requirement at this point. The key to success in racing manufacturing is still being able to come up with a creative solution to a problem that results in the car being able to go faster. If you can do that, you will be in demand. One way to get some experience with engines, for example, is to volunteer to work on a local race team. If you have some success at that level, you will soon have the chance to move up.

POSITION: Facilities

EDUCATION: Degree in liberal arts, business.

SALARY: Intro: $18,000
                  Average: $40,000
                  Top level: $100,000

JOB DESCRIPTION: Racing facilities around the country run the gamut from dirt ovals used every Fourth of July to multipurpose tracks that host a series of major events all year round. They hold crowds of anywhere from a few hundred people to the hundreds of thousands at the Indianapolis 500 every year.

The smaller facilities use part-time, often volunteer, help. But the major tracks have full-time staff people involved in the planning and execution of the racing schedule through the year.

Unlike stadiums and arenas, most racing facilities are privately owned. They are therefore looking to generate a profit, which means the more days of racing at the track, the better. This in turn leads to an increase in the number of jobs available.

Types of jobs at facilities include general management, marketing, public relations, concessions/hospitality, track maintenance, ticket sales, and security, as well as the general business functions such as accounting and finance. Most tracks operate or are involved in a number of side ventures besides racing, such as renting the facility for testing, hosting driving schools, or leasing garage space around the facility.

Jobs in facility management offer a measure of security not common in racing. Your job does not depend on winning, or on the sponsor signing up for another year, or on someone renewing your contract. If the job you do is important enough to the operation, you will have the chance to do it year in and year out, no matter how attendance fluctuates or how many races get rained out in a season.

Compensation for jobs at a racetrack is comparable to jobs with professional teams—for the most part, below average. There are people standing in line for the opportunity to "be involved" with racing, as in all sports, which tends to keep salaries and benefits down. But as more and more people with professional backgrounds enter motor sports, and as motor sports continue to grow in popularity as a marketing strategy for national brands, the level of expertise required to do an effective job for a facility will rise. Salaries and total compensation packages will be sure to follow.

Getting a job at a racing facility is similar to getting a job with a professional team. Sometimes internships are available. Many people get their start with a facility by first becoming a member of the part-time or seasonal staff. During the summer months especially, most tracks hire a large number of seasonal employees. Those who demonstrate the most promise during the summer racing season or during the planning and execution of a particularly large event will be asked to stay and work at the facility year round.

POSITION: Manufacturer's representative

EDUCATION/TRAINING: Technical expertise, product
knowledge a plus.

SALARY: Intro: $25,000
Average: $40,000
Top level: $75,000

JOB DESCRIPTION: A manufacturer's representative is just that—a person who is paid by a manufacturer to work with its customers, sell them its product, give them information, troubleshoot problems, handle complaints and suggestions, and build good relationships. The world of racing is filled with opportunities to be a manufacturer's rep, since the number and variety of products used in and around racing is very large.

The job of the manufacturer's rep depends on the product represented. One can generalize somewhat, however.

A manufacturer's rep is in charge of a sales territory. A territory may be as small as a single client company or may cover many states in an entire region of the country. The rep is responsible for all of the sales and marketing activity taking place in that region. He certainly has to know all of his customers, and must also know who all of his prospective customers are. Most of the time the job involves direct selling, showing the client the latest line, replacing inventory, and trying to generate new orders. Some of the time it involves no selling at all, but is more of a public relations effort to insure that the client is getting what he needs from the manufacturer.

In racing, manufacturer's representatives often work for companies that produce equipment, things such as tires, brakes, engine components, and so on. They deal directly with the race teams, trying to get them to use their products. If a car wins the Indy 500 using Quaker State Oil, Quaker State becomes the oil of champions for the year. On a local level, if the number 7 car wins the weekend sprint week after week, and it is running on Goodyear tires, the fans and certainly the other drivers are going to take notice. Plus, hard-running racing cars can consume a lot of a product. These are the kinds of considerations a manufacturer's rep deals with.

Other manufacturer's reps get involved with racing as well. Auto manufacturers have huge regional sales forces, many of whose members spend a lot of time working in one kind of racing or another. The same goes for parts makers, oil companies, beer companies, tobacco companies, and others. Even Procter & Gamble goes racing, with its Tide brand. And all of them have regional representatives involved in their racing program.

Besides selling, it is often the job of the manufacturer's rep to entertain clients at races. This can be as simple as getting a couple of tickets and pit passes and taking a customer out for a day at the track. Or it can be as elaborate as arranging for a covered hospitality area for 500 people along the race course, complete with a barbecued steak lunch, an open bar, and an appearance by Rusty Wallace to sign autographs. It is all part of building a relationship with the client, developing a trust and a friendship that will lead to better business dealings in the future.

Most manufacturer's representatives get to travel quite a bit, don't have to sit behind a desk eight hours a day, and have the freedom to decide what they are going to do each day. They are also under pressure to perform. It is hard to defend why your territory is down twenty-five percent in sales when the two neighboring territories are up thirty percent. But if you work well on your own, like to work with people, and know how to sell, the job of manufacturer's representative can be a great career choice.

Getting a job as a manufacturer's representative takes a lot of homework. You must identify the companies that have representation in your area and those that you would be interested in working with. Go to races and see which companies are involved. Talk to a few of the reps in your area—take them out to lunch or buy them a beer at a race. Get to know what they do and the channels you have to go through to get started with their company. Better still, get in touch with the person who supervises the reps in your area. These are usually high-turnover jobs, and supervisors are always on the lookout for a qualified replacement. Keep your goal in mind, and don't limit yourself to one company, one industry, or one part of the country. The more flexible you are, the better your chances for ultimate success.

POSITION: Marketing

EDUCATION/TRAINING: Degree in business, marketing, or advertising preferred.

SALARY: Intro: $20,000
                  Average: $40,000
                  Top level: $150,000

JOB DESCRIPTION: Marketing positions are plentiful in racing. The reason for this is that racing is decades ahead of other sports in using the sport to sell products. Think of how long STP has been "The Racer's Edge." Companies have been touting the victory of cars at the Indy 500 that use their products since the thirties. This has led to the creation of a variety of jobs in marketing in all facets of racing. Marketing positions exist with teams, drivers, facilities, sponsors, single events, national and regional sanctioning bodies, and even with independent agencies that do nothing but racing marketing.

The job of marketing is defined in many ways. Overall, it is probably best defined as the process of identifying a target audience and communicating a message to them. This message is most often sales related, but can be image building or informational as well. In racing, just about every person that you will ever meet who hands you a business card that has "marketing" in his or her title wants to sell something to somebody.

Marketing jobs exist both inside the sport and outside. By that I mean there are a lot of marketing jobs that are essential to the business of professional racing. These jobs include creating effective advertising campaigns to get the public out to the racetrack for big events, creating a high level of interest to sell tickets, and making the sport big enough and popular enough to attract major sponsorship and media dollars. These jobs are comparable to marketing positions with franchised sports teams. They deal with getting people in the seats and generating revenue.

Even more marketing jobs exist "outside" the sport. These positions don't have a direct impact on who races from week to week, but in the long run can be even more important to the sport. This category includes marketing positions with sponsor companies, or suppliers, or manufacturers, or any of the number of companies that sell to racing fans or that use racing as a marketing tool. These are the people who make decisions on which car to support, which driver to hire as a spokesperson, how to use racing at the retail level with sweepstakes, contests, and so on, and how much advertising revenue to spend on broadcasts of racing. Many companies have senior-level marketing directors who spend millions of dollars every year on racing. Through the design and execution of their marketing plans, these directors and their marketing staffs determine whether the money is well spent or not.

Jobs in racing marketing, especially the top-level corporate jobs, require a solid educational background. Many require an MBA. Entry-level jobs include account coordinator positions at advertising or marketing companies, brand assistants with major manufacturers, or assistant marketing positions at facilities. Again, internships are very helpful in eventually landing a job. So are part-time positions. Since racing is seasonal in most parts of the country, seasonal marketing positions are often available. Also, promoters often can use some part-time help in marketing major events, such as when CART, the NHRA, or NASCAR comes to town. By taking advantage of these opportunities, you will develop the expertise and the network of racing contacts needed to get a full-time marketing position.

POSITION: Media relations

EDUCATION/TRAINING: Degree in journalism; excellent writing skills.

SALARY: Intro: $15,000
                 Average: $35,000
                 Top level: $75,000

JOB DESCRIPTION: It seems like everyone in racing has a "PR person." The track has a PR person. The event has a PR person. The team has a PR person. The sanctioning body has a PR person. The sponsors have several PR people. Even the drivers have PR people. The journalists covering racing have no trouble getting all the help they need to compose this week's story.

The reason so many people are working in publicity in racing relates to the length of time corporations have been using the sport to market products. They have discovered over the years that if you have a full-time person working for you in the area of publicity, your name gets in the paper more often, it is spelled correctly, information you want to get out is included, and information you don't want to get out can sometimes be minimized.

Because sponsorship and product identification have been a part of racing for so long, journalists who cover racing are much more sophisticated in this area than their counterparts in other sports. First of all, they don't make up a bunch of silly rules about not using corporate names on the air or in print. If the event is the Coca-Cola 600, they call it that, not "a stock car race in Charlotte, North Carolina." Bill Elliott drives a Ford, not an unnamed car. They call things as they and the fans see them; they don't play games. Part of this also relates to their realization that without sponsor mentions in the media, sponsors wouldn't be involved in racing. And without sponsors, racing wouldn't exist—and neither would the need for journalists to cover racing. They are therefore open to suggestions from public relations people. If someone has a good story idea, they'll run with it and give everyone the proper credit.

Not all public relations people are out to get someone's name in print, of course. Many are employed just to help the media do their job more easily. They compile background information on each team and driver, hold press conferences, arrange interviews, run down answers to technical questions, and in general act as an information source for journalists. This allows the media to get the story out better, faster, and more accurately to the fans, to the benefit of everyone.

It is a fact that sporting events are media-driven. There may be 100,000 people at a race every year. But this year it's REALLY big, because CBS is here! If it's on network TV, it MUST be big! By helping the media do their job, the public relations director can add to that feeling of bigness, and at the same time help make sure the information that gets out is correct, timely, and fair.

Getting a job in racing public relations requires a good background in writing or journalism, a feel for how the media works and what they are looking for, and a thorough knowledge of racing. A good way to begin is to volunteer to help in the pressroom at a local event. While making copies, taking notes during press conferences, and running the fax machine, you will be able to talk with members of the press and get a feel for what it is all about. Another way to start is to develop an internship for yourself. Some groups, like the NHRA, have programs set up for young people to get some experience in this area. Other organizations, especially sponsoring companies, may have internship programs set up in other areas of their business that you can adapt to public relations and racing. If your writing is good enough and you can get along well with the members of the media, enough of this experience will nearly guarantee you a job in racing public relations.

POSITION: Crew

EDUCATION/TRAINING: Expertise in automobile or engine manufacturing and operation; college degree preferred for top jobs.

SALARY: Intro: $15,000
Average: $40,000
Top level: $1,000,000

JOB DESCRIPTION: Becoming a member of a racing crew is not difficult. Getting a lot of experience as a member of a racing crew is also not tough. Just go to an amateur race at your local track, look for a driver doing his own "wrenching," tell him that you'd like to help, that you know what you're doing, and that, by the way, the beers are on you at the end of the race, and bingo, you're on a crew.

The hard part is getting paid to do it. And the really challenging part is making a career out of it.

Racing equipment is so sophisticated and the money involved today is so large that professional teams in many kinds of racing have full-time, year-round crews. Not that many years ago, even top-flight circuits like NASCAR used to include a lot of weekend warriors, people who had other jobs and just worked races for fun on the weekends. Now these kinds of teams are few and far between in any kind of top-level professional racing, and they almost never win.

To get a job as a professional racing crew member takes either years of experience at lower levels—learning the ropes, meeting the people, and gradually moving up—or very particular expertise in areas teams need help in. Examples of the kind of expertise that will get you a job on a team are experience with computers, especially relating to measuring and interpreting performance; working with new engines; and working with new auto bodies. Of course, in order to have gained this kind of expertise, one would have had to either study it extensively in school or have worked somewhere else. If I was running an engine program for the first time, the first person I would hire is the person who put it together. His total personal racing experience may be go-carts in the third grade, but he knows that engine and how to generate horsepower, and horsepower wins races.

Even now, most of the time crews are formed by word of mouth. "My guy is leaving, do you know somebody who's any good?" "Yeah, this guy has been calling me and I heard he's all right, but I can't use him so here's his number," and that's how it happens. But even in today's competitive environment, if you have developed the skills and the expertise at lower levels of racing, and if you bring innovation, creativity, and leadership to the table, you can be on a crew in no time at all. You don't need to be anyone's nephew, your father doesn't have to be named Unser, Andretti, Petty, or Allison. It takes a lot of legwork, contacting teams and owners. But the bottom line in racing is, if you can deliver the goods, the job is yours.

POSITION: Publications

EDUCATION/TRAINING: Degree in journalism.

SALARY: Intro: $20,000
Average: $35,000
Top level: $75,000

JOB DESCRIPTION: Racing is one of the few sports in this country that supports a lot of different publications. From *National Dragster* to *Speed Sport News*, the various circuits and races are chronicled in a host of regional and national publications. Excluding the "buff magazines" like *Car and Driver* and *Motor Trend*, there are more than twenty different publications around the country that focus on automobile racing. Additional magazines like *Sports Illustrated* and *Sport* include racing as part of their regular general sports coverage.

Working for a racing publication usually requires a strong knowledge of racing coupled with the ability to wear a couple of different hats. During races, you may be at the track covering the race, interviewing drivers, and generating stories. You may also be required to take pictures for the story. Then, back at the office, you may have to edit your own copy and also edit a few other stories for the next edition.

Besides writing and editing, publication jobs can involve management of advertising sales, circulation, promotion of the publication, marketing, public relations, as well as a host of jobs in the actual printing and distribution process. Some publications have a staff of only a handful of people. The biggest ones, like *National Dragster*, have over forty full-time employees.

Other jobs in the publishing area are found with the people who produce the souvenir racing programs. These publications are distributed at racetracks all over the country. For racing series like NASCAR and CART, each individual event is responsible for producing its own program. The national sanctioning body provides it with some help in the way of national advertising, stories, features, photos, and statistics. The rest is produced locally by the facility or the promoter. Many promoters contract all or part of the program production out to a private producer. A typical contract will require the producer to give the promoter, say, 10,000 finished programs by a certain date. The producer sells all of the advertising space in the book and gets to keep the revenue. Many people in racing publishing got their start by writing, editing, and selling advertising for souvenir racing programs.

Getting a job in racing publishing is much the same as getting any job in journalism. It requires developing your writing ability to the fullest, building a reputation, and then selling your skills to a magazine or newspaper. Ways to start that process include working as a stringer at racing events, writing racing stories for smaller publications or newspapers, or working in the public relations department at a major racing event. Since most newspapers don't have a full-time person assigned to racing, calling newspapers in a racer's hometown and offering to provide a story or two about him might land you an assignment. Once you have a few features to show editors, you are on your way.

POSITION: Sales

EDUCATION/TRAINING: No specific requirements.

SALARY: Intro: $15,000
Average: $25,000
Top level: $100,000

JOB DESCRIPTION: Sales as a job category is tough to define—and tough to ignore. Many jobs in marketing, facilities management, public relations, and with sponsors require selling of some sort or another. But that is just the point: if you can sell, you can get a job in racing.

Sales jobs in racing start at race events, with the sale of souvenirs, programs, and concession items. Jobs also exist in sponsorship sales; selling signage at the racetrack; program advertising; selling local, regional, and national radio and television time; and selling hospitality areas and catering services. And of course, there is the whole area of ticket sales to consider. At small facilities or where racing is very seasonal, these kinds of sales jobs are part-time at best. But by working at major racetracks, or following the top racing circuits, or working at smaller tracks that operate year round, a salesperson can earn a very good living and take in as much racing as he or she would want.

Getting a sales position is relatively easy, especially if you are willing to work on commission. This means that you don't get a salary, or get a very small one, but that for every sale you make you receive a percentage of the profits. If you don't sell anything, you don't make any money. But if you sell a lot, there is no limit on how much money you can make.

To get a sales job in racing, it is important to be able to work with people, to have a good appearance, and to be hardworking and personable. You will also need to know everything about your product, depending on what you are selling.

For example, if you are selling hospitality areas, you will need to know who has what locations already booked (putting Coke next to

Pepsi won't work). You need to know how big the spaces are and what kind of access to the pits they have. Customers will want to know how many toilets are included, what kind of tents, fences, and carpeting they can order, and about the different menu choices they have for their food service. They'll also ask about power, lights, heaters, and air conditioners. The list goes on and on. You are the expert. And by helping the customer make informed choices, the salesman can maximize the revenue generated by the sale.

Jobs in sales require stamina and a bit of a thick skin. When you get turned down for the tenth time, you have to be able to pick yourself up that eleventh time and make your pitch.

Your first selling job, selling yourself, is best accomplished by talking with the person on whom your efforts would have the greatest impact. This person may be a director of sales at a racetrack, a regional sales manager, or a promoter. If you can convince that person that hiring you will lead to more sales, you will be on your way.

POSITION: Sponsor

EDUCATION/TRAINING: College degree usually required.

SALARY: Intro: $20,000
Average: $40,000
Top level: $250,000 plus

JOB DESCRIPTION: "Sponsor" in this case refers to that broad group of businesspeople who spend money on racing. They don't have "sponsor" on their business cards. Their jobs are really positions in management, or marketing, or advertising, or media buying. But in racing, being a sponsor means something so special that we are treating it as a separate job category.

As mentioned, racing is an older, more sophisticated sport in many ways. One of the main ways is the fact that everyone in and around the sport recognizes the fact that racing on the highest levels exists because of corporate sponsorship. Without the millions of dollars generated from sponsors, racing research and technological advances would dry up, and eventually the whole sport would be downgraded. So if you work for a sponsor, no matter what you do, you are appreciated. And if you work for a major sponsor, you are revered.

What are sponsor jobs? Most of them are the ones we have described, in areas such as public relations, marketing, sales, management, customer relations, and advertising. Some are strictly racing jobs, working with the sanctioning body or a series of racetracks to make sure your sponsorship benefits are accrued and that you take full advantage of the opportunity. Others deal with taking the sponsorship to retail, creating giant Danny Sullivan cutouts to put by the display at the grocery store, creating sweepstakes contests with a trip to the Indy 500 as first prize, or arranging a one-hour autograph and photo session with the show vehicle and driver at a shopping mall. The more the sponsor is committed to racing, the more and the wider variety of jobs it offers. Some companies employ twenty people or more, just to manage their involvement in racing.

To get a "sponsor racing job," you need to do one of two things: Either develop your expertise in a specific area that fits the sponsor's needs or go to work for the sponsoring company in another capacity and change departments. The first way is the best way. It gets you directly where you want to go, without running the risk of getting stuck somewhere in the company you'd rather not be. Getting this kind of job again depends on doing your homework, identifying a company's needs and trying to fill them, networking within the racing community to find out who needs what, and being flexible. If you don't care what part of the country you end up in or what company you work for as long as it is stable, fair to its employees, and involved in racing, you will be way ahead of the game.

WHERE THE RACING JOBS ARE: These jobs are located where racing takes place. This means primarily in the East, the Southeast, the Midwest, and California. Stock car racing dominates the Southeast. But there is racing of some sort in every state.

KEYS TO GETTING THE JOB:

• Strong educational background.
• Experience, attained by volunteering or working at small facilities and one-time events, and internships.
• Thorough understanding and affection for racing.
• Specialized skill development in areas such as engineering, design, computers, marketing, and public relations.

CLUBHOUSE MANAGER

POSITION: Clubhouse manager

EDUCATION/TRAINING: No specific educational requirements, but a college degree is preferred.

SALARY: Intro: Minimum wage, game days only
Average: $40,000
Top level: $150,000 (including playoff bonus)

JOB DESCRIPTION: The clubhouse manager has one of the most unique jobs in sports. He is the individual who works in the home and visiting clubhouses, or locker rooms, in the Major League Baseball stadiums around the U.S. and Canada.

Each team in baseball has two clubhouses, one for the home team and one for the visiting team. Each of these clubhouses has a manager. The manager in turn has a staff of several people who help him on a part-time basis.

The home team manager takes care of his clubhouse and the home team players every game, while the visiting team manager takes care of the various visiting teams that come through town during the baseball season.

The duties of home clubhouse managers vary somewhat from stadium to stadium and team to team. In essence, they are responsible for seeing that each player is equipped and ready to step out on the field for every game. They order the player's bats, make sure his uniform is clean and ready every day, do the player's laundry, make sure there is a supply of baseballs on hand. They even make sure the player's shoes are cleaned and look sharp. In a way, this part of the job is like being a baseball butler for two dozen people.

Before each game, the clubhouse manager will put out a supply of snacks and food items such as candy, sunflower seeds, coffee, and soft drinks for players and coaches to munch on. After the game, the clubhouse manager makes a full meal available to the players, including special requests. The clubhouse manager is also expected to provide any toiletries the players need, such as shampoo, conditioner, mousse, hairbrushes, and combs.

The home clubhouse manager travels with the team, making sure that all of the players' equipment and personal items get to their proper destination at the hotel or the ballpark when the team is on the road.

In addition, the home clubhouse manager serves as an information clearinghouse for the players. He knows their families and friends, and is the one who gets messages to the players from their wives, fields some of the inquiries for appearances by the players, and in general acts as a buffer between the players and the general public.

The visiting clubhouse manager has very similar duties, except for the fact that he services a different set of players every few days. The visiting clubhouse manager sees to equipment and laundry once the team has reached the ballpark. He, too, puts out a variety of food and snacks for the players and serves them meals after the game. In many cases, the visiting clubhouse manager will provide special meals for those players he knows have special likes and dislikes. After a few years in the league, he gets to know what teams and individuals prefer, and can treat them accordingly.

Compensation for clubhouse managers varies a bit from team to team. In general, the home clubhouse manager is paid by the team and also receives some tips from players for doing them special favors. The visiting team clubhouse manager charges the players for services rendered and also receives tips from the players. Taking care of the clubhouse managers is one of the unwritten laws of baseball—every player is billed for services but is also expected to kick in a little extra, especially when someone goes out of his way to do the player a favor. When Reggie Jackson was playing, he sometimes requested a lobster dinner for after the game. When he got what he wanted, he tipped accordingly.

Teams that go to the playoffs and World Series earn money from a bonus pool. This pool is divided among the players and whoever else they choose to include, at their discretion. Clubhouse managers are often included in this dispensation. Today, if the clubhouse manager is voted a full share, the amount of money he receives is over $100,000.

WHERE THE JOBS ARE: Major and minor league baseball teams across the country.

KEYS TO GETTING THE JOB:
* Experience in baseball, gained through playing or working in a clubhouse as a seasonal helper. Send letters to teams in your area asking if they need anyone. Be persistent.
* Just like the players, clubhouse managers move up from lower levels of the minor leagues to the majors. It is very important to build good relationships with players and coaches along the way.
* Good organizational ability.

COACHING

POSITION: College coach

EDUCATION/TRAINING: Degree in education, sports administration; master's degree for schools where teaching classes is required.

SALARY: Intro: $20,000
Average: $35,000
Top level: $1,000,000 plus

JOB DESCRIPTION: In a lot of sports, college play is the highest level of competition available. Except for a few men's sports like football, basketball, baseball, and hockey, professional team sports either do not exist in this country or are fledgling operations. Even in Olympic sports like gymnastics, swimming, and track and field, college is the place most of the coaches work day to day. And in women's athletics, the highest level virtually across the board is college coaching.

The job of a college coach varies greatly with the size of the institution, the sport, and the expertise of the coach. Large, Division I athletic programs can support a host of head and assistant coaches who just coach. In National Association of Intercollegiate Athletes (NAIA) programs, it is more common to find coaches who also teach classes as part of their contract. Football coaches generally do not get involved in much besides coaching. Archery coaches almost always do.

The job of the college coach is to help the student athletes in the program reach the highest level of success they can. That means improving their skills, and it also means winning. In major college programs, the job of the tennis and soccer coaches is the same as the job of the football and basketball coaches—to compete well and to win. While a lot of times this creates undue pressure on the coach, it is what is expected. After all, if a coach does a good job at what he is supposed to do—recruit and train athletes—he will have success. If the coach doesn't do a good job, the results are obvious on the scoreboard.

Coaching at the college level is really teaching: helping athletes learn about physical training, working with them on technique during practice, devising game strategies to help them overcome their opponent. The students are unpolished, and can have entirely different skill levels from one another. But through the teachings of a good coach, they can gradually improve and achieve success.

Becoming a college coach has its prerequisites. First of all, just about every college coach has competed on the collegiate or professional level in the sport he or she is coaching. It is rare for someone to jump from the chem lab to coaching lacrosse in college without having played the game at that level. Second, it takes a strong educational background. To get hired, coaches need a college undergraduate degree, and many of them have graduate degrees. Third, especially in the revenue sports such as football and basketball, it takes some experience. Fortunately, most college sports have fairly clearly defined pathways for those interested in the field.

For example, take the career of Don James, head football coach at the University of Washington. Don played quarterback for Miami of Florida, setting five school records and graduating with honors. After two years in the military, he went to graduate school at the University of Kansas, where he also coached the freshman football team. After obtaining his master's, he returned to Miami and coached high school football and basketball. He then took a job as an assistant football coach at Florida State. After a few years, he rose to the position of assistant head coach and defensive coordinator. After a dozen years as an assistant at a couple of schools, Don was hired as the head coach at Kent State University. After four years there, he accepted the job at Washington.

The pattern in football coaching today is the same. Get the educational background, coach at lower levels such as high school or become a graduate assistant, move up to assistant coach, then to head coach at a smaller school, and eventually become head coach at a big school. For other sports as well, high school or assistant coaching in a good college program is still the best way to get started and to build the reputation you will need to get a good college job.

WHERE THE JOBS ARE: Colleges and universities across the U.S.

KEYS TO GETTING THE JOB:
• A college degree in physical education, education, or coaching; priority given to those with master's degrees.
• Coaching experience at lower levels.
• Playing experience in high school or college.

POSITION: Private coach

EDUCATION/TRAINING: Advanced technical expertise.

SALARY: Intro: $20,000
Average: $40,000
Top level: $100,000

JOB DESCRIPTION: A private coach is someone who works with an individual athlete to help him or her reach full potential. Private coaches work primarily in individual professional or Olympic sports, such as tennis, golf, gymnastics, and figure skating.

The job of the private coach is to do what it takes to help the athlete achieve an ultimate goal. No one hires a private coach with a goal of making the cut at the U.S. Open golf championships. The coach is hired to help the athlete WIN the U.S. Open.

Whether the goal is a gold medal or a world championship, the coach is the person responsible for getting the athletes where they want to go.

Day after day, the private coach teaches technique and helps with training; pushing, pulling, and cajoling better and better performances out of the athlete. The job requires a thorough knowledge of the sport and coaching techniques, plus the ability to build a relationship with the athlete. Sometimes success in sports is as much mental as physical. The private coach must address this mental aspect of performance and be able to come up with ways to motivate and inspire the athlete.

Getting a job as a private coach boils down to how much confidence the athlete has in your abilities. Normally, confidence and respect for your ability to coach come from your being a leader in your coaching field and being innovative, with a long track record of helping athletes succeed. This is accomplished by working on a high school, collegiate, or club level, doing a good job, and establishing a reputation. Once you have demonstrated a high level of expertise, you can begin networking with other coaches, trainers, and administrators of national teams and elite athletes. With a proven track record and familiarity with the people at the top level of the sport, it will only be a matter of time before you get the chance to work with someone as a consultant or private coach.

WHERE THE JOBS ARE: Individual sports such as tennis, golf, swimming, diving, figure skating, and gymnastics, and some team sports for skill development, such as basketball or football.

KEYS TO GETTING THE JOB:
• Expert ability to coach.
• A good deal of coaching experience.
• Ability to motivate.
• Ability to work intimately with one or two people for a long stretch of time.
• A reputation for helping athletes solve problems with their game or perform at a higher level.

POSITION: Professional team coach

EDUCATION/TRAINING: Professional playing career; college
coaching background.

SALARY: Intro: $35,000
Average: $60,000
Top level: $1,000,000 plus

JOB DESCRIPTION: Coaches in professional football, basketball, baseball, and hockey either come from the ranks of college coaching or are former players who go straight from competition to professional coaching.

The job of the professional coach is to win. In some cases, even winning is not enough; you must win championships. The job consists of building the kind of team you think you can win with and then working with it to achieve that goal. For the most part, coaches are working with athletes who make a lot more money than they do, and who in the long run are more valuable to the franchise, or indeed the league, than the coach will ever be. This makes the job of motivating the athlete that much tougher.

A big part of the job is preparing the athletes to compete, both physically and mentally. Teaching is replaced by the fine-tuning of skills already learned. Professional baseball players have been bunting since they were in Little League, but they still spend time on it every spring training. Batting coaches work on helping hitters identify the pitch they should hit. Pitching coaches work on setting up batters and getting ahead in the count. In short, they help the players refine the little things in their game that in the end make the difference between winning and losing.

Professional head coaches are the highest-paid coaches in the country, and are among the highest-paid in the world. With endorsements, incentives, and bonuses, they can make over $1,000,000 per year.

WHERE THE JOBS ARE: Franchise sports teams in the U.S. and Canada.

KEYS TO GETTING THE JOB:
• Successful professional playing career.
• Background in college or minor league coaching.

POSITION: Strength and conditioning coach

EDUCATION/TRAINING: College degree in exercise science, education, biomechanics, kinesiology. Master's degree required for top positions.

SALARY: Intro: $25,000
Average: $40,000
Top level: $110,000, plus bonus potential

JOB DESCRIPTION: The newest position in coaching is the strength and conditioning coach. Strength coaches are responsible for taking care of "well" athletes. They help them with weight and aerobic training, flexibility, speed and quickness exercises, and even give them information about diet and nutrition.

More and more emphasis in every sport is being placed on properly preparing to compete. Sports like boxing and baseball used to cling to the old theory that weight training would make you bulky, inflexible, and slow. Today, boxers and baseball players are among the most vocal advocates of the benefits of a comprehensive conditioning program.

Strength and conditioning coaches are getting hired at colleges, by professional sports teams, and as independent consultants to individual athletes. With the dramatic increase in sports salaries and other revenue opportunities for successful athletes, more and more of them are looking for ways to extend their careers, minimize injuries, and increase performance. The teachings of a good strength and conditioning coach can help them reach those goals.

Getting a job as a strength and conditioning coach starts with a good educational background. This includes at least an undergraduate degree in one of the physical education disciplines. A master's degree is even better.

Entry-level jobs are available with colleges, as assistant coaches, or even on the high school level. These positions will most likely carry with them some teaching responsibilities. From there, the progression is to head conditioning coach at a college and on into the professional ranks. While most conditioning coaches are former athletes, that is not necessarily a requirement for this coaching position, especially since the bulk of the jobs are in colleges. Being a former football player does not help much when you are building a program for the women's swim team.

WHERE THE JOBS ARE: Professional sports teams in the U.S. and Canada; Division I and many lower-division college teams; some high school programs; with individual athletes.

KEYS TO GETTING THE JOB:
• Strong academic background in the exercise sciences.
• Credibility, established through a successful competitive career or coaching success at a lower level.
• Experience as a graduate assistant at the college level.

COLLECTOR

POSITION: Collectibles manufacturer

EDUCATION/TRAINING: Experience/expertise in print production, retail sales.

SALARY: Intro: $15,000
Average: $30,000
Top level: $100,000

JOB DESCRIPTION: The world of collectibles, especially baseball cards, has exploded in the last five to ten years. Cards, autographs, and memorabilia have become a big business.

The high level of interest in collecting has led to an increase in the number of job opportunities available. Some of these, like becoming a card show promoter or opening a retail store, don't really fit the criteria for inclusion in this book. Opening a card store is no different from opening a doughnut shop. You lease a location, get the product, and sell it. Same with being a card show promoter. You lease a building, rent out tables to collectors, do some advertising, and you are a card show promoter.

The part of collecting we will look at is card manufacturing. There are eight or nine major card manufacturing companies doing business in the U.S. today, companies like Donrus, Topps, Upper Deck, and Fleer. As these companies expand, they will need more and more people to help them in a variety of areas.

Baseball cards started out as a vehicle to sell products like chewing gum and cigarettes. As more and more people started collecting them, the cards became more valuable than the product. Because of these early beginnings, though, card manufacturers are still set up as a combination of food and printing companies.

The larger card manufacturers can have 500 employees or more.

Most of these people work on production and distribution of the product. Many of them are unskilled workers who cut and package the cards for sale. There are a number of other opportunities within the company, however.

Card manufacturers have photographers on staff to take the pictures of the athletes. For baseball, they travel to team sites during spring training and take the pictures for that year's set of cards. Marketing and public relations specialists help build interest in the cards, and develop the points of difference between their cards and their competitors'. Staff artists design the look of the cards, and researchers assemble and verify the information for the backs of the cards. Customer service representatives work with collectors to answer questions and solve specific problems with the product. And the sales force works with the brokers who distribute the product to the stores.

Keep in mind all the steps it takes to get the trading card produced and in your hands, and that will give you an idea of the variety of jobs available with these companies. Photos need to be taken, the backs need to be written, and it all needs to be printed on cards, which must be packaged, shipped to stores, and sold. Many manufacturers are also in the mail-order business, which creates other job opportunities. Provided that the interest in cards is not a passing fad, this will continue to be one of the major growth areas for jobs in sports in the country.

WHERE THE JOBS ARE: Major metropolitan areas, corporate headquarters cities: Fleer is located in Philadelphia; Donrus is in Fort Washington, Pennsylvania; Topps in Brooklyn; and Upper Deck in Yorba Linda, California.

KEYS TO GETTING THE JOB:
• Knowledge of the printing business or photography.
• Knowledge of the retail sales/brokerage business.
• A keen interest in the sport the target company produces cards for, most likely baseball, but also football, basketball, or hockey.

COLLEGE ATHLETICS

POSITION: Athletic director

EDUCATION/TRAINING: Degree in liberal arts. Preference given
to candidates with a master's or Ph.D.

SALARY: Intro: $45,000
Average: $70,000
Top level: $200,000, plus such perks as housing, cars,
and retirement funds.

JOB DESCRIPTION: The job of athletic director is the top position
in college sports administration. The athletic director is the CEO of
the athletic department. All of the coaches and the entire staff work
for him. He is in control of the budget. It's not unfair to say that the
overall success or failure of a college athletic program depends
on him.

The responsibilities of the athletic director, unlike other jobs in
college sports, don't vary much with the size of the department.
Whether a school is NAIA Division II or NCAA Division I, the job
is more or less the same. In a nutshell, the job of the athletic director
is to provide student athletes with the facilities and opportunities to
compete at the highest level of their ability. This means using whatever funds are available to hire the best coaches, play the best
competition, and buy the best equipment he can. Larger schools may
compete in more sports and have much larger budgets, but the basis
of the AD's job is still the same.

At larger universities, the athletic director may administer a budget
in excess of fifteen million dollars and host a million fans or more
over the course of a year's events. The AD must also deal with the
complex nature of today's college sports scene, raising money from
alumni, insuring that athletes are making satisfactory progress toward

a degree, keeping the program from running afoul of NCAA regulations, giving coaches what they need to recruit top athletes, and doing it all within the confines of an educational, often state-run institution.

It is a tremendous challenge, much like running a small corporation, yet often the financial compensation pales in comparison to other senior sports management positions. While the general manager of an average professional baseball team may make $400,000 per year, a top AD may make $60,000. The trade-offs are the high level of prestige you have within the community and the opportunity you have to work with kids.

Getting a job as an athletic director starts in school. Most athletic directors start their careers as educational administrators. In the college environment, this almost always requires a master's degree, and in many cases a Ph.D. in education or sports administration. Once you have established your credentials, you can apply for jobs around the country as an assistant or associate athletic director and move up from there.

An example of a typical career as an athletic director is that of Andy Geiger, athletic director at the University of Maryland. Geiger decided when he was a sophomore in college at the University of Syracuse that athletic administration was for him. At that point, he joined the department as an intern, doing a little bit of everything and learning as much as he could. Upon graduation, he took a coaching job at Dartmouth. The following year, he found out about an opening as assistant athletic director at Syracuse. Since the school was familiar with him and his work, he got the job. He worked at Syracuse in that role for six years. From there, he joined the East Coast Athletic Conference as the junior administrator. He was heavily involved with coaches, officiating, and especially the rowing program. While working for the conference, he found out about an opening for, and was subsequently hired as, athletic director at Brown. After that, he served as AD at Penn and Stanford, and now is at the University of Maryland. This demonstrates a fairly average career pathway. He started early, working in school, then moved to different jobs in order to move up the career ladder, each time gaining a little more responsibility and controlling a bigger budget.

The job search system in education is fairly well developed, with job openings being posted through state employment services and in academic and athletic publications. One note: to date, only two women have ever been named athletic director at major, Division I universities that have football as a revenue sport. Perhaps this book will be able to contribute to changing that situation.

KEYS TO GETTING THE JOB:
• Good educational background.
• Experience in college administration as an assistant or associate athletic director.
• Strong management and budgeting skills.

POSITION: Associate athletic director

EDUCATION/TRAINING: College degree required; master's, Ph.D. preferred.

SALARY: Intro: $30,000
Average: $45,000
Top level: $75,000

JOB DESCRIPTION: The associate or assistant athletic director is the "middle management" level between the various department heads and the athletic director. This level may not even exist in the smallest programs, but the larger ones may have five or more administrators in these positions.

Associate athletic directors are primarily managers, making sure the departments they are responsible for operate smoothly, within budget, and within the guidelines set by the college and the other governing bodies. Typical departments managed by associate ADs are finance, sports information, university relations, operations, and fund-raising. It is their job to keep the AD informed at all times, solve the problems they can, and manage and motivate their employees.

KEYS TO GETTING THE JOB:
- Experience in managing people.
- Strong educational background.
- Expertise in a specific area of sports administration, such as finance, ticketing, NCAA rules and regulations, or marketing.

POSITION: Booster club coordinator

EDUCATION/TRAINING: Degree, often from college you are representing.

SALARY: Intro: $17,000
Average: $40,000
Top level: $65,000

JOB DESCRIPTION: The job of booster club coordinator is really an alumni relations position, but it has a narrower focus. College booster clubs are groups of alumni who band together to support the athletic department financially and to have some fun with college athletics. Since these contributions are a significant part of an athletic department's fund-raising effort, an administrative position is sometimes formed to work with the alumni on a day-to-day basis.

Support from booster clubs can run in the millions of dollars every year for an athletic department. It is the job of the booster club coordinator to see that these boosters are recognized for their contributions, that they have organized opportunities to interact with the players and coaches on the teams, and that they have fun.

It is also the coordinator's responsibility to make sure the booster club does not get carried away and that it operates within NCAA guidelines covering the recruitment and treatment of student athletes. The past decade has been filled with stories of abuses in this area, with college boosters paying athletes, providing them with cars and apartments, and generally ignoring NCAA rules. After a few major programs were dealt with severely (most notably at SMU, where athletics were suspended for a year), colleges and booster clubs started to get the message. Today, it is the booster club coordinator's job to make sure everyone involved with the club knows and follows NCAA guidelines.

To get a job as booster club coordinator requires some experience in athletic administration, perhaps gained through an internship, but more importantly it requires expertise in the area of fund-raising. That is, after all, the main function of the booster club from the school's perspective. Fund-raising expertise can be gained by working for any of a number of nonprofit organizations. Couple this experience with a good understanding of NCAA rules, and you will be qualified for this kind of job.

A common misconception is that simply knowing a lot of alumni supporters and being part of that group qualifies you for this kind of job. It really doesn't. Anyone who gets the job of booster club coordinator will eventually get to know all of the donors. That's how it works. The important prerequisites are the management and fund-raising skills. The rest will follow.

KEYS TO GETTING THE JOB:
• Educational/administrative background.
• Creative ideas for fund-raising and activities.
• Knowledge of NCAA or NAIA rules governing alumni/booster activity.
• Familiarity with booster club programs.

POSITION: Conference administration

EDUCATION/TRAINING: Degree in business, liberal arts; master's and Ph.D. given preference.

SALARY: Intro: $15,000
            Average: $40,000
            Top level: $150,000

JOB DESCRIPTION: In Division I college athletics, most of the colleges and universities are grouped into conferences. These conferences have their own administrative staff positions.

Jobs that typically are available with the conference are in public relations, broadcasting, enforcement and compliance, officiating, marketing, and championships administration.

The public relations department handles conference publicity, keeps track of statistics and standings, and produces publications for the conference members. The size of the department can range from one person to four or five, with part-time positions and internships included. Most conference public relations directors have come from the ranks of college sports information directors.

The broadcasting department works with radio and television networks on securing rights fees and producing broadcasts of regular-season, championship, and bowl games. Since these rights fees are by far the largest source of income for the conference, this is obviously crucial in today's college sports environment, and usually involves not only a broadcasting director but the executive director and even a committee of conference members to manage. As cable becomes a bigger factor in college athletics, the number of conference broadcast director positions will continue to grow.

The enforcement and compliance department works with the NCAA and conference schools to make sure the members are following the guidelines and are using eligible players, and investigates all charges of wrongdoing leveled against them. A typical career pathway in this field is that of Duane Lindberg of the Pacific Ten Conference. Duane received a master's degree in sports administration. While pursuing his degree, he served as an intern with the Pacific Ten Conference. After graduation, he joined the conference in the area of public relations. After spending a few years in PR, he moved to the compliance area as assistant director. He then went to the Southwest Conference as director. He is currently back at the Pac-10 office, serving as assistant commissioner.

Officiating handles all of the recruiting, training, scheduling, transportation, and expenses of the various referees, officials, and umpires needed at conference events. Unlike the administrators at the conference level and above, those who officiate college events are part-time employees. They get paid on a per-game basis, and have other jobs that support their families. Maintaining a pool of qualified officials is one of the most important, and one of the most overlooked, responsibilities of the conference. The people who work in this area are for the most part former or current officials who started by working their way up the ranks from junior high officiating through high schools and community colleges to get to where they are today.

Marketing departments work with member schools to promote college athletics, and specifically conference championships, throughout the conference area. They are also responsible for securing corporate sponsorships and endorsements and generating outside revenue for the member schools.

Finally, championships administration: Conferences have championships in many different sports throughout the academic year that need to be coordinated. Sites for the championships need to be found, extra officials need to be hired, and the events need to be publicized. The conference championships administrator works with the host schools to make sure they cover all of the bases and that the events come off smoothly.

Overseeing all of these departments is a commissioner, responsible for all conference activities. The commissioner manages all of the people on the conference staff, creates and oversees the budget, handles television negotiation and contract management, is closely involved with the officiating department, and works with the member colleges' presidents, athletic directors, and other officials in setting conference policy. The commissioner is also very involved with the conference governing body, the NCAA or the NAIA, serving on committees and helping shape the face of college athletics.

Commissioners attain their position in one of three ways. They either work their way up through the ranks of conference administration, sometimes changing conferences in order to move ahead, or they come from a governing body like the NCAA or NAIA, or they join the conference after serving as athletic director at a member school. Of these, the most common are the first two.

Conference staff sizes range tremendously, from one or two people to twenty or more. Their size depends on the number of schools involved and the scope of their programs, with the biggest conference staffs being those like the Big Ten, the Southeastern Conference, and the Pacific Ten, whose members are major universities competing in football, basketball, and a host of minor sports.

KEYS TO GETTING THE JOB:
- Gaining familiarity with NCAA rules and regulations.
- Picking up experience at a member institution.
- Doing an internship with the conference you are interested in working for.

POSITION: Counseling

EDUCATION/TRAINING: Degree and experience in academic counseling.

SALARY: Intro: $12,000
Average: $25,000
Top level: $45,000

JOB DESCRIPTION: Many athletic departments have counselors affiliated with them, separate from or only loosely connected with the regular college counseling service. These counselors help student athletes form their academic schedules, arrange for tutors and study sessions, and work with the admissions department on determining the eligibility of incoming recruits. Some are also responsible for arranging for athletes' summer jobs. The coach helps them with their athletic life; the counselor helps them with their academic life. It is no secret that some athletes, just like some members of the regular student body, could not get through college without some help. The difference is, the college or university has a major investment in the athletes, and is more anxious to help them stay in school and keep them eligible to compete. The counselor is there to make sure that help is available.

Becoming an academic counselor for athletics is no different from becoming an academic counselor for the student body in general. The requirements are a degree in education, with an emphasis on academic counseling. From there most people join the regular college counseling department to get some experience. It is sometimes possible in these roles to work on special projects with the athletic department, such as setting up a special tutorial program. Once you have some experience and have shown special interest and ability in the area of counseling athletes, you will be a good candidate for the next opening in that area.

KEYS TO GETTING THE JOB:
- Strong educational background.
- Academic counseling experience.
- Good relationship with faculty and staff.

POSITION: Enforcement/compliance

EDUCATION/TRAINING: College degree; thorough knowledge of NCAA or NAIA rules and regulations.

SALARY: Intro: $20,000
Average: $35,000
Top level: $70,000

JOB DESCRIPTION: Every college program in the country has on staff someone with the responsibility of making sure the athletic department is operating within the rules of the NCAA, the NAIA, the college, and the conference. This person has a complete understanding of all of the rules and regulations the college athletic program needs to follow, including all of the latest changes and interpretations. Should a violation be suspected, the enforcement director conducts an investigation and makes a report to the governing body involved, along with recommended penalties.

While this may appear to be more of a police job, it is really a job of communication. Very few coaches or athletes want to break the rules or get into trouble. Because the rules are so complex, however, they may do something that seems okay but is actually a violation. The main job of the compliance director is to see that everyone—coaches, staff members, athletes, and alumni—knows the rules and follows the guidelines set down by the governing body. The job of director of enforcement is often combined with other responsibilities. As the rules get more and more complex, however, the need grows for someone to handle this area full-time.

The job is primarily administrative in nature, with a great deal of time being spent interacting with athletes, the governing bodies, the coaching staff, and the college or university administration. Preparation for this job includes obtaining a degree in sports administration, preferably a master's. It then requires expert knowledge of the rules and regulations of the governing body. The best place to get that is by actually working for the NCAA or the NAIA in the enforcement department. The second choice is to combine these responsibilities with other duties as a member of an athletic department and to learn on the job. Again, as the federal and state governments take closer and closer looks at higher education and athletics, college presidents will feel more and more pressure to control their own programs. This will only lead to a growth in job opportunities in this area.

KEYS TO GETTING THE JOB:
• Knowledge of rules, regulations, and guidelines.
• Some experience with enforcement and compliance procedures, gained by becoming an intern or perhaps working for the NCAA or the NAIA, or by serving as an assistant compliance director at the conference level.

POSITION: Equipment manager

EDUCATION/TRAINING: College degree preferred.

SALARY: Intro: $17,000
Average: $30,000
Top level: $45,000

JOB DESCRIPTION: The equipment manager is responsible for buying, maintaining, and keeping track of all of the equipment used by the athletes to practice and compete.

The amount and variety of equipment needed is staggering. Consider that the professional sports, such as baseball, have someone handling the equipment for that one team full-time. Imagine having squads in baseball, football, hockey, gymnastics, track and field, and a dozen other sports, all with athletes who need the equipment year round to practice. It is an organizational challenge, to say the least.

Equipment managers usually have a fairly large number of student volunteers to help them, which eases some of the burden. Much of their job becomes budget and inventory control and the management of their assistants. Just as in professional sports, the equipment manager has a great opportunity to get close to the athletes and to really feel like an important part of the competition.

The career pathway for an equipment manager usually starts in college. Most equipment managers began by helping out part-time in their college athletic departments. They then joined those departments as assistants and worked their way up from there.

KEYS TO GETTING THE JOB:
• Starting early in your college career, either by volunteering or working part-time.
• Familiarity with sporting equipment.
• Ability to work with a budget.

POSITION: Facilities management

EDUCATION/TRAINING: College degree, often in architecture or engineering.

SALARY: Intro: $20,000
Average: $40,000
Top level: $70,000

JOB DESCRIPTION: Colleges' athletic facilities are getting larger, more diverse, and more expensive to build and maintain. Years ago, a large grass field for outdoor sports and a gymnasium for indoor sports were all that was needed to host a full range of athletic programs. Now, schools have huge stadiums for football, venues for basketball and baseball, swimming pools, indoor and outdoor tennis facilities, special areas for weight training, and as many as a dozen grass and artificial-turf fields. Building, maintaining, and operating all of these is the job of the facilities manager.

At a typical college, the facilities manager's job is to make existing buildings and facilities last, to handle remodeling when it is necessary, and to head all new construction projects should the money be found to start them. He and his staff are in charge of preparing all the facilities for competition, from dragging the infield of the baseball diamond to cutting the grass for the field hockey tournament.

The job today requires a good deal of expertise in the areas of architecture and engineering, as colleges seek to add facilities and to improve existing ones without hiring additional staff members to do the job. Unlike their professional counterparts, college facilities managers cannot afford to specialize in one area. They are required to know just as much about resurfacing a basketball floor as they do about resodding a soccer field. It is this variety, and being forever "in season," that is part of the appeal of this job.

The facilities manager usually has a lot of help at his or her disposal, mainly regular college maintenance staff people. The school has on board a number of electricians, plumbers, carpenters, and general maintenance workers who can work on the press box as easily as on the chemistry lab. But because of the special nature of college sports, and the demands placed on the facilities during an event, there is at least one person, and often many more, working on athletic department projects exclusively.

Like many jobs in college athletics, the best way to start in this field is by helping out while you are in college. This can be in the guise of an internship or part-time job, or just as an interested volunteer. The areas to especially key on are budgeting, people management, and work with subcontractors and college staff members on building projects. If you can be a part of a project from beginning to end, from planning to dedication, you will gain a great deal of experience that can be applied later, when you receive your degree. It doesn't matter if the job is putting in a new basketball arena or a new tennis court. By studying the process, you will learn the basics of what you need to know for any project. Once you have this experience and the degree to go with it, you will be a good candidate for a job in a college operations department.

KEYS TO GETTING THE JOB:
• Strong educational background.
• Engineering or architectural experience.
• Construction/maintenance project management experience.
• Experience at college sports facilities, gained by working part time or volunteering as a student, or through an internship program.

POSITION: Fund-raising

EDUCATION/TRAINING: Degree in business or liberal arts.

SALARY: Intro: $22,000
Average: $40,000
Top level: $60,000

JOB DESCRIPTION: As the pressure to balance athletic department budgets grows, so does the need for athletic department fundraisers. Raising money is a difficult, time-consuming task, no matter what the cause. Today, hospitals, arts organizations, political parties, schools, and many other nonprofit charities make use of professional fund-raisers. Athletic departments have jumped on the bandwagon in the past decade.

Effective fund-raising for athletics takes solid planning and a lot of effort. Every person in the department is involved, under the direction of the staff fund-raiser, from the athletic director to the coaching staff.

The money comes from many and varied sources: corporations,

individuals, estate planning gifts, foundations and granting authorities, and social events such as auctions, walk-a-thons, and dinners. Developing and coordinating these activities and maximizing their potential to raise funds, constitutes the bulk of a fund-raiser's job. It is very time-consuming, as there is always one more alum to meet, one more cocktail party to attend, one more game to watch with a corporate VP. But it is very important to the success of the athletic department, and offers new challenges every day.

Getting a job in fund-raising for an athletic department requires a degree, usually in sports administration. Internship programs in this area are available at most colleges, either in the athletic department or with the college fund-raising department. Also, it is easy to get experience in this area by volunteering to work on a series of fund-raising events for your college athletic department. Contact your local director of fund-raising to see how you can help.

Finding a permanent job in this field requires some searching and enough flexibility to go where the jobs are. Look in one of the college and university publications that list job openings in athletics, or contact your local college director of fund-raising for recommendations. It is a fairly close-knit fraternity, and its members communicate often.

This is a relatively new position in college athletics, one that more and more colleges are currently trying to add to their staff. Given schools' tremendous need to discover and exploit new sources of revenue, now is a good time to enter this particular field of college athletics.

KEYS TO GETTING THE JOB:
• Degree in sports administration.
• Background in working with nonprofit organizations.
• Familiarity with the community, prominent alums, business leaders.
• Creative, low-cost fund-raising ideas.
• Willingness to work long hours, weekends.

POSITION: Health care

EDUCATION/TRAINING: MD, DDS, appropriate degrees and licenses.

SALARY: Intro: $15,000
Average: $50,000
Top level: $200,000 plus

JOB DESCRIPTION: There are about as many kinds of links between the health care profession and college athletic departments as there are universities. Some colleges have medical schools and hospitals on campus, and the athletic department uses those services. Others have some professionals on staff, and contract for the rest of their needs. It is this latter kind of relationship that creates sports jobs.

Health care professionals usually don't limit their practice to collegiate athletes. The number of patients they would see in a year would not be large enough to generate significant revenue. Nevertheless, most colleges in the U.S. have established a relationship with specific medical doctors, therapists, dentists, and optometrists. While this may not be the largest part of a practice, it is a very significant part of it. If you are the doc who fixes the knees of the football players for State U., patients will seek you out. The job of team doctor, dentist, and so on is therefore very desirable.

The role played by these health professionals is largely the treatment of injury. Work in preventative medicine and training is handled by others on the staff. If an athlete is going to see the team doctor, he or she is either sick or hurt. In fact, most of the time the doctor is a specialist in orthopedic medicine, a surgeon capable of repairing the wide variety of knee, hip, shoulder, ankle, and elbow injuries athletes receive while competing.

Direct compensation for these jobs is fair to low compared to the industry average. The health professional is most often under contract to the athletic department for a fee, which may be adjusted depending on the amount of services rendered. The real rewards are being able to work with the athletes, performing state-of-the-art, showcase procedures, and the large amount of referral business that is generated through association with the teams.

KEYS TO GETTING THE JOB:
• Being a leader in your field of health care.
• Willingness to put the needs of the college athletes ahead of those of other patients in your practice.
• Availability to travel with the team and attend all events, as needed.

POSITION: Marketing

EDUCATION/TRAINING: Degree in business, liberal arts. Master's degree in marketing or sports administration preferred.

SALARY: Intro: $17,000
                   Average: $35,000
                   Top level: $50,000

JOB DESCRIPTION: In the never-ending pursuit of revenue, college athletic programs are becoming more and more sophisticated in the area of marketing. This includes such things as generating revenue from the local broadcast of games on radio and television, selling school merchandise, selling tickets to events, creating special events, advertising, doing public relations, doing research on the people who come to games, involving local or national sponsors, and in general treating college athletics like a product that needs to be packaged and sold. Colleges have for years been leaders in the area of publicity, but have lagged far behind sports and the entertainment field in other marketing disciplines. They are just now starting to catch up.

The marketing director is typically responsible for generating all revenue for the athletic department. Sometimes, fund-raising and ticket sales are split off and covered by someone else, but most of the time they fall under the area of marketing.

The marketing director has to maximize exposure for the teams and athletes, create an atmosphere of excitement to boost ticket sales and ratings, and do it on as small a budget as possible. The money for the production and airing of television ads to promote the basketball team, for example, just isn't there. It is a constant challenge, finding new and imaginative ways to build the business and keep costs down.

Eventually, every major college athletic program and many of the smaller ones will include a marketing specialist on staff. The competition for the entertainment dollar is too fierce to rely on the loyalty of fans and the performance of the team on the field. Once this happens, the field will open up dramatically.

Obtaining a marketing position requires first fulfilling the academic requirements of the position. It is helpful to also get some experience, most likely obtained by serving as an intern in a college athletic department or a professional team. Entry-level positions are usually in promotions or as an assistant to the marketing director. Jobs in this area are also posted in the various NCAA and NAIA publications.

KEYS TO GETTING THE JOB:
• Strong educational background.
• Some experience in sports marketing, either as an intern, volunteer, or in a previous job.

POSITION: Recruiting coordinator

EDUCATION/TRAINING: College degree; coaching background.

SALARY: Intro: $17,000
Average: $30,000
Top level: $70,000

JOB DESCRIPTION: The recruiting coordinator may be the one who makes the greatest contribution to the success of an athletic program. He supplies the athletes. Without championship athletes, even the best coach cannot produce champions. This function is so important, athletic departments now hire staff members whose sole job is to find and persuade high school and junior college athletes to enroll at and compete for their school. This person, the recruiting coordinator, works with his staff and the coaches, administrators, and professors to accomplish this goal. Even current and former students get involved in the process.

The recruiting coordinator at smaller schools often has many other duties, such as teaching classes or coaching a sport. At larger universities, especially ones that play Division I football, recruiting coordinators stick to recruiting year round. The job consists of staying in constant touch with high school coaches in your recruiting area, looking at miles and miles of film and videotape to evaluate athletes, and talking to kids, coaches, parents, neighbors, teachers, and whoever else you can contact to get information on an athlete. You become an expert on how an eighteen-year-old athlete decides which college to attend. It requires a lot of organization, plus the ability to communicate with kids and parents from a wide variety of backgrounds and possibly from all parts of the country.

It also takes the talent to evaluate athletes. Looking into the future and projecting how good an athlete and how good a student a seventeen- or eighteen-year-old kid can become in five years is tricky business. Kids this age have a lot of growing yet to do, both physically and emotionally. Recruiting coordinators use a lot of predictors like grade-point average and test scores for how they will do in school, but on the athletic field there are no such predictors. The recruiting coordinator has to rely on experience and gut feelings. An inexact science, to be sure.

Finally, the job requires a lot of patience. Patience to be able to adjust to the whims of the young adult who can't seem to make up his mind about what day it is, let alone where to spend the next four or five years of his life. Patience to be able to deal with the coaching staff, who hold the recruiting coordinator responsible when they are a kid's second choice or when a player from their area goes out of state to school. And patience to take yet another call from well-meaning high school coaches, alumni, and parents who can't understand why a particular student hasn't been offered a scholarship yet.

For the most part, recruiting coordinators concentrate on the revenue sports—football and basketball. Most recruiting coordinators come from the ranks of high school or college coaches in those two sports. They have spent many years evaluating the talents of high-school-age athletes. They know how to tell when a high school coach is inflating a player's accomplishments to help him or her win a scholarship. They have also established a lot of contacts with high school coaches and administrators, contacts that are essential when trying to determine who to look at and who to pass on.

If you have some coaching experience and are interested in this type of position, especially in football, the key is to tap into the "recruiting network." This is the unofficial network of college coaches and recruiting coordinators across the country. Just as in college coaching, jobs in recruiting are filled more through recommendations from peers than by anything else.

The way to start is by helping your local college recruiter as an evaluator. An evaluator is a person who looks at the huge amount of videotape a recruiter gets each year and identifies the athletes who can someday play at the college level. If you prove good at this, and identify some kids who prove to be winners, you will already be on your way to building the kind of network of friends and contacts needed to land a job as recruiting coordinator.

KEYS TO GETTING THE JOB:
• Coaching, teaching experience at the high school or college level.
• Experience in evaluating athletes.
• Strong organizational skills.
• Strong communication skills.

POSITION: Sports information (public relations)

EDUCATION/TRAINING: College degree; ability to write well.

SALARY: Intro: $12,000
Average: $35,000
Top level: $60,000

JOB DESCRIPTION: Sports information, or public relations, is one of the most established positions in college athletics. Working with the press to chronicle collegiate athletic achievements has been a paying position in athletic departments for over a century. Today, sports information is often the largest division within the athletic department, with full- and part-time employees numbering in the dozens.

The head of this group is the sports information director, the SID. The SID needs to be an expert in three areas: media relations, publishing, and personnel management. The job consists of equal parts of all three.

It is the SID who arranges for all of the interviews between student athletes and the media, juggling class schedules and availability of coaches to accommodate newspaper deadlines and television air-times.

The department is also responsible for all of the printed materials produced about the teams and athletes, from press releases to media guides to game programs and, often, such things as team posters and schedules. The large amount of this material that is produced requires the SID and his staff to have great writing and editing skills, and to be able to turn things around very quickly.

Staff management is another key to success for the SID, especially at schools that play Division I football. The sports information staff at a football game handles all of the activities in the press box. This includes taking and distributing statistics at each quarter, announcing the game, working with the play-by-play announcers, conducting postgame interviews, providing people to run the copy machine, sending faxes, hooking up phone lines, and answering the needs of a press corps that can exceed a hundred people. To meet the needs of the media effectively requires a lot of people, most of whom are students, volunteers, or game-day-only employees. The SID must find the people needed to do the job, train them, and plug them into various roles as needed.

As anyone in college athletics will tell you, the people in sports information work the hardest for the least amount of money. They always have teams in season, most of the time three or four. They have games, meets, or matches to cover just about every day and every night. Even if the media are not present, they want the results of the competition and someone to talk to who was there. It means very long hours, little time off, and weekends full of football from August through December and basketball from November through March.

It is also the most diverse job in college athletics, and is second only to athletic director as a stepping-stone to other jobs in sports. Sports companies, professional teams, television networks, agencies, and media outlets look for qualified job candidates in college sports information offices around the country. The list of former SIDs in other sports jobs is huge, probably headed by former NFL Commissioner Pete Rozelle, who was the SID at the University of San Francisco. It is a great training ground, and if you can stand the hours and live with the salary, it enables you to get close to the athletes, coaches, fans, and journalists who make college sports so enjoyable.

Getting a job as a sports information director starts with a degree, usually in journalism or communication. This is supplemented by some experience in the area, which can be obtained by volunteering at games or special events. As described before, there are many part-time or day-of-game jobs available in this department. Also, most colleges can arrange internships. After you have gained some practical experience, you will be ready to start looking at entry-level positions in sports information, which usually have titles like assistant sports information director.

KEYS TO GETTING THE JOB:
• Journalism training/background.
• Public relations training/background.
• Willingness to work long hours.
• Enthusiasm for all teams and sports, not just football and basketball.
• Volunteering or working part-time on game days to get exposure within the department.

POSITION: Strength and conditioning coach

EDUCATION/TRAINING: Coaching; nutritional education;
                                kinesiology.

SALARY: Intro: $20,000
                    Average: $30,000
                    Top level: $50,000

JOB DESCRIPTION: In the last ten years, the job of strength and conditioning coach has evolved at lightning speed. Led by colleges like the University of Nebraska and professional teams like the Oakland A's, athletes in all sports are using weight training, nutrition, flexibility exercises, aerobics, and other sophisticated training techniques to enhance their performance. Because of the success of these programs, and the level of expertise needed to develop effective, individualized training programs for male and female college athletes, the position of strength and conditioning coach was created.

Strength and conditioning used to be ignored, or, in the best programs, was the responsibility of one of the assistant football coaches. Weight training was done only by football players. Today, athletes in all sports, men and women, are involved in weight training year round..The strength and conditioning coach is an expert on the kinds of training and nutrition needed to swim faster, wrestle better, perform tougher gymnastics moves, and hit the curveball for power. He may still coach a sport, but his main focus is on helping all the athletes in a program reach their potential and avoid injury. Training facilities costing millions of dollars are being built in colleges around the country to accomplish these goals.

In order to become a strength and conditioning coach, you must have a thorough knowledge of the body, be familiar with the latest training techniques, and have a good understanding of the benefits of nutrition. Whereas in the past the jobs were taken primarily by former athletes, the field has become so technical in nature and the stakes so high for universities and athletes that a strong academic background is now the first priority. After getting the proper academic training, the place to start is as an assistant strength and conditioning coach on the college or professional level. Since this is a relatively new field, new jobs are opening up in colleges and even in high school districts every year for those who are qualified.

KEYS TO GETTING THE JOB:

- Scientific background/training. The field is changing so rapidly, those without a solid academic foundation are being left behind.
- Ability to work with a wide variety of athletes, both male and female, in a wide variety of sports.
- Experience in teaching and motivating kids.

POSITION: Tickets

EDUCATION/TRAINING: Business, accounting degree.

SALARY: Intro: $15,000
Average: $30,000
Top level: $40,000

JOB DESCRIPTION: The backbone of the budget for any athletic department is ticket sales. Even the smallest schools sell tickets to their events. The largest ones generate millions of dollars of revenue that way. Keeping track of all these tickets and accounting for all the revenue is the job of the ticket manager.

The size of the ticket staff varies greatly with the institution. Those schools with large facilities on campus or that run off-campus operations require staff members for season-ticket, individual, and group sales. This includes a number of full-time people as well as part-time student help and volunteers.

The ticket sales administrator manages all of the inventory, mainly for revenue sports such as football and basketball. He coordinates with other departments to put together ticket plans for corporate accounts and boosters, and manages all of the personnel involved. He is also responsible for setting up communication channels for the fans, from direct-mail campaigns to walk-up windows and telephone numbers to call with requests and complaints. As is typical with tickets, the complaints outweigh everything else two to one. It requires a thick skin, patience, and the ability to handle pressure.

As the selling of tickets has become more computerized, the number of people required to manage the job has decreased. Emphasis has shifted away from simple ticket transactions and accounting to the development of effective strategies and tactics to generate revenue from tickets. This includes designing a variety of season-ticket packages and sales materials, using advertising to market the events, working with outside ticket vendors to increase availability of tickets, and putting together a team to solicit season, group, and individual sales.

Ticket sales is a real behind-the-scenes job. It has little glamour, and receives practically no attention until problems arise. But the ticket seller is the only representative of the college athletic department who the average fan will ever meet or talk to in person. For that reason, it is crucial for the ticket manager and his staff to be professional and courteous at all times—not an easy task when someone is asking you for the fourth time why he can't sit behind the bench this year.

Getting a job in tickets usually begins with selling from behind a window during an event. Just about everyone who is in the business of tickets started by selling them, either in a volunteer, full-time, or part-time position. It is preferable to work in season-ticket selling or in customer relations, since most of the other ticket jobs are clerical in nature and will not teach you very much. Once you have established yourself, keep asking for more duties and opportunities to get further involved. In tickets, especially during busy times, you can often take on a frighteningly large amount of responsibility simply by asking for it. And from there, how far you go is up to you.

KEYS TO GETTING THE JOB:
- Experience in working with cash transactions.
- Attention to detail.
- Experience with tickets. To get it, volunteer or work part-time during particularly busy times, like when season tickets are mailed

out or the two weeks before a bowl game, or work on ticket sales for minor sports.
• Ability to work with computers.
• Customer relations skills.

POSITION: Trainer

EDUCATION/TRAINING: Degree in physical therapy; licensed trainer.

SALARY: Intro: $18,000
Average: $35,000
Top level: $45,000

JOB DESCRIPTION: At the turn of the century, the trainer was the person who coached college athletes. By the thirties, coaches did the coaching and trainers handled physical conditioning. Today, these activities are handled by strength and conditioning coaches. The trainer of the nineties is more of a medical practitioner, concerned with two areas: injury prevention and rehabilitation.

A trainer's work on injury prevention starts with making sure the athletes are physically able to compete before they start. This can run the gamut from making sure a bothersome ankle has been taped to keeping an athlete out of competition because treatment is incomplete. While most people see trainers as the people who apply the ice packs and help the athletes into the whirlpool, they are actually the hands-on extension of the college medical staff. Combined, they have the final say on who competes and who doesn't.

Once an injury occurs, the trainer becomes even more involved with the athlete. A treatment program is designed for the athlete, and the trainer and his staff make sure it is executed. They are experts in rehabilitation, knowing how much to push a recovering athlete and when to back off. Most of the time, the patients they deal with can't believe they weren't indestructible and have no patience with a gradual rehab schedule. It goes against their grain. They think that if working on a knee injury for fifteen minutes is good, a half hour must be better and an hour would really be something. They don't know that too much too soon can do even more damage. It is the trainer's job to see that they do enough, that they push themselves but don't go too far.

Not all of the trainer's work is done in a locker room or training area. A lot of work is done at the sporting event, during the heat of the moment. Split-second decisions and quick action taken by the trainer can make a difference in a game. If a star basketball player turns an ankle, a quick ice pack application and tight tape job can perhaps put him back in for the second half. A pitcher gets hit on the wrist by a batted ball; the trainer may be able to take one look at it and decide the pitcher is done for the day. The athlete may protest, but will be able to pitch another day instead of causing a more severe problem. And at a football game, the trainer is constantly busy looking after bumps, bruises, sprains, and more severe injuries like broken bones and concussions, deciding what to treat, how to treat it, and looking out for the welfare of the player.

Becoming a trainer requires specific courses of study. In many states, trainers must be licensed in order to practice. Unlike other health care givers, trainers are usually employees of the college, and are members of the athletic department staff. The permanent staff of trainers may be augmented by physical therapists under contract or by part-time trainers and assistants who work during football season only.

The typical career pathway for a college trainer is to start as a part-time or volunteer assistant while still in school, move up to become a paid graduate assistant at the end of your training or after graduation, and then take a job as a full-time assistant trainer. Following a few years as an assistant, you will be ready to assume the duties of a head trainer.

KEYS TO GETTING THE JOB:
• Educational background, degree in physical therapy, biomechanics, exercise physiology preferred.
• State license, if required.

• Experience in injury prevention and treatment.
• Familiarity with sports medicine.

POSITION: Video services

EDUCATION/TRAINING: Degree in television or communications.

SALARY: Intro: $12,000
Average: $25,000
Top level: $35,000

JOB DESCRIPTION: The newest job category cropping up in college athletic departments across the country is director of video services. This person is responsible for managing the use of videotape in the department.

Videotape has replaced film as the medium used to record and evaluate the performance of athletes. In football, for example, the video services director tapes all practices and games. He can then put the raw footage into any form the coach or athlete may want it in for study. The quarterback coach may want to look at a compilation of every throw his player has made while running to his right. The defensive backs coach might want to isolate all the plays his cornerbacks made in man-to-man defense. From this, the coach and the player can learn a great deal about their performance and tendencies, and use that information to improve.

Football is probably the most advanced sport in the use of video. But all sports use it to some degree. Athletes in swimming, track and field, tennis, and golf can use video to make the minor corrections in their form and technique needed to make a difference. Basketball and volleyball teams can use it to work on play execution. And of course, videos of opponents are broken down and studied in all sports, revealing weaknesses to exploit and strengths to stay away from.

When the amount of video use and the time needed to shoot and compile all of the tape requested began to become overwhelming, some schools devoted a full-time staff member to the job. Now, virtually every major athletic department has someone responsible for video services.

Becoming a director of video services starts with a degree in communications or television or whichever department at your college teaches you how to use video equipment and do editing. The next step is getting some practical experience with the athletic department. This can be done on a volunteer basis or as a part-time job, taping practices and editing for coaches. The video department is usually staffed by only one or two people, and they can use all the help they can get during the busiest times of the year. Once you have received your degree and have some experience under your belt, you are ready to put together your sample tape and enter the job market. The best way to break in is to find either a small college where you can run the video program (probably in conjunction with some other duties) or a university that would hire you as an assistant.

KEYS TO GETTING THE JOB:
• Ability to operate video equipment: cameras, editing machines, and so on.
• Being able to edit. Shooting the tape is a much smaller part of the job than editing. If you are a good editor, and fast, you will be much more valuable.
• Many schools have video equipment they will allow students to use, sort of as on-the-job training. Take advantage of the situation to practice your skills.
• Availability. If football practice conflicts with a baseball game, the video services director will need help to cover both events. If he knows you are a phone call away, you'll get the job. You'll gain experience, and also become familiar to members of the athletic department.

POSITION: Women's athletic administrator

EDUCATION/TRAINING: College degree; master's or Ph.D. preferred.

SALARY: Intro: $25,000
Average: $45,000
Top level: $100,000, plus perks and bonuses

JOB DESCRIPTION: Title IX changed women's collegiate sports forever. This legislation required colleges to spend the same amount of money on women's programs as they do on men's. In the course of a year, many colleges added half a dozen or more sports for women. In the beginning, women's athletics were not under the control of the NCAA. They had their own national governing body. At the school level, this led to the creation of a parallel athletic department, set up to handle women's sports. At the top of this department was the women's athletic director.

Today, men's and women's sports are under one governing body. But a number of schools still have separate leadership for men's and women's athletics. The top executive in women's athletics is called the women's athletics administrator.

The women's administrator is usually a senior executive, reporting to the athletic director. All women's sports fall under her control. The job to be done is more or less the same as the men's administrator's, with one major difference. Almost without exception, women's programs do not generate enough revenue to support themselves. They must be supplemented by funds from the men's program or from the college. In today's world of tight budgets for college athletics, women's sports budgets are the tightest.

However, lack of big budgets has also meant a lack of big problems. Recruiting violations are rare. Athletes compete for the fun of it, to be the best they can, since they have no professional contract to look forward to. Women still have the same pressure to win, coaches still get fired for poor records, and kids still lose their eligibility for skipping class. But the women's administrator is able to spend more time working with budgets, building competitive schedules, and raising money, and less time on press conferences, ethics investigations, and agent tampering.

At schools where the department is still split, women's administrators make about the same money as athletic directors and are eligible for the same perks. At schools where all athletics are under one person, they usually have the title of senior associate athletic director and are paid accordingly.

KEYS TO GETTING THE JOB:

• It helps to be a woman. While many coaches of women's teams are men, colleges feel senior administrators for women's athletics should be women.
• Experience in budgeting, planning, and managing.
• Excellent fund-raising ability.
• Past participation in women's athletics, as a coach or player.

COMMUNITY SERVICE

POSITION: Charitable organization manager

EDUCATION/TRAINING: No specific requirements; college
degree preferred.

SALARY: Intro: $20,000
Average: $30,000
Top level: $60,000

JOB DESCRIPTION: Many charities use sports teams and celebrities in their fund-raising and publicity efforts. If the involvement is
significant enough, the organization may have on staff one or more
people devoted entirely to this effort.

The job of managing the sports marketing activities of a charity
varies greatly from organization to organization and city to city.
However, some of the activities you could get involved in are acting
as the host charity for a PGA golf tournament, working with NFL
players at a pro-am golf event, developing tie-ins with radio and
television stations that carry games, or creating promotions where
you receive money, say, for each home run hit or goal scored.
Frequently, charity managers work directly with athletes or their
wives, either on specific projects or as part of a general affiliation
the athlete and his family have with that charity. Athletes may
participate by agreeing to head fund-raising drives, by acting as
talent for television and radio public-service announcements, by
lending their name to golf and tennis events—whatever works in a
given community to raise awareness and money for the charity.

Getting a sports job with a charitable organization first requires
doing some homework. If the charity is one that is already involved
in sports, such as the Special Olympics, or is tied in with a sport,
such as the arrangement between United Way and the National

Football League, it is likely to be headed by people who like that affiliation and want to make it grow. Organizations that have never done anything with sports shouldn't be totally discounted as prospects, but the chances are remote that any substantial involvement could happen right away.

As a general rule, charities are always on the lookout for people with enthusiasm and fresh ideas about fund-raising. If you have a college degree and a viable plan for making money by combining sports and a charity, you will have no trouble getting people to listen to you and landing a job.

WHERE THE JOBS ARE: Big cities across the United States, specifically with major United Way charities.

KEYS TO GETTING THE JOB:
• College degree.
• Interest in sports.
• Experience in fund-raising.

POSITION: Team community service director

EDUCATION/TRAINING: No specific background required; college degree preferred.

SALARY: Intro: $20,000
                  Average: $35,000
                  Top level: $60,000

JOB DESCRIPTION: Most of the teams in the major professional sports leagues and a lot of the major facilities have at least one person in the area of community service. The job of the community service director is to act as a liaison between the team and the various charitable, nonprofit, educational, and other special-interest groups in the community that care about the team.

A professional sports team is seen as a community asset. What happens to that team and its players is recorded in the newspaper, on radio, and on television every day, not just as an afterthought but with whole sports sections, color photos, and live remote interviews. The highly visible nature and wide-ranging popularity of a team comes with a responsibility to the community in which it plays. Therefore, for a lot of the right reasons and occasionally for the wrong ones, a huge number of groups in the community want to work with the team and its players, usually to enhance their own image or to lend credibility to their projects.

It is the job of the community service director to work with these groups, to determine which ones to associate with and how to do it, to devise a plan, and to act upon it. Projects are wide-ranging. Food drives. Library reading incentive programs. Stay-in-school messages for kids. Entertainment programs for senior citizens. Player appearances at hospitals. Speeches by players at business and social clubs. The list is endless.

The community service director is trying to accomplish certain objectives. First and foremost of these is to build a bond between the team and the community. Showing that the team and the players care enough to donate a lot of time and money to help crippled children is an example of the kind of things that can be done to build a bond.

The second goal is to carry out team or league specified directives. Many team owners have devoted themselves to a particular cause for a long time, and want the team to follow suit. Also, leagues such as the NBA and the NFL have formed relationships with particular charities, and require their members to participate in certain programs surrounding this affiliation.

The third objective is to take some of the community service load off the players. While everyone has the best intentions at heart, players are constantly and often unfairly hounded to make appearances, give clinics, or sign merchandise for auction. For even the most giving player, it can quickly become overwhelming. The need will always outstrip what he has to give. By one person's coordinating the requests for help, more of the right groups end up getting what they want, and everyone is treated fairly.

The job of community service director can be a lot of fun and very rewarding, helping a lot of different people in a lot of different ways. It is also trying at times, calling for tough decisions to be made. If you raise $50,000 for the children's hospital, how can you turn down the request for help from the Cancer Fund? How do you explain the reason why a player can do a public-service announcement to help fight AIDS one week, but can't do one to support fighting lung cancer the next? Or the week after that? It's tough. But someone has to make and carry out those choices, and that someone is the community service director.

Most community service directors for teams start by working for a charity. This gives them the experience they need to discern what qualifies as a contribution for tax purposes, how to work with volunteers, and what kind of events work in that community to raise money, and enables them to make the contacts with radio stations, newspapers, and businesses that they'll need once they join the team. Some other community service directors come from education, either as former teachers or administrators. These people have a good understanding of how to access kids through the educational system, and what kinds of things kids need. But the bottom line is, if you have a good knowledge of your community and some experience in working with nonprofit organizations, you can be a candidate for this kind of position.

WHERE THE JOBS ARE: Major league sports franchises and facilities.

KEYS TO GETTING THE JOB:
• Familiarity with nonprofit organizations.
• Creative fund-raising ideas.
• Good contacts within the community.

COMPUTER SPECIALIST

POSITION: Computer specialist

EDUCATION/TRAINING: Degree in computer science;
operational experience.

SALARY: Intro: $15,000
Average: $25,000
Top level: $40,000

JOB DESCRIPTION: Sports, like all other business ventures in the country, are depending more and more on computers to perform essential tasks. From payroll to player personnel, computer programmers, operations specialists, and data processors are finding opportunities with sports teams and facilities.

Just about every sports organization today uses computers for things such as word processing, payroll, accounting, and budgeting. For those organizations that sell tickets, new ticketing software packages come on the market every year. These finance and ticketing jobs alone require a computer specialist to design the system, train users, and troubleshoot. But in sports, the computer is used for much more.

At the major league level, and even in some minor leagues, most teams have a computer specialist on staff to manage the use of computers in the area of scouting and player personnel. These computers are used to store and evaluate information on players in the league and on prospective players still in college or high school. Programs are created to ease the tracking of athletic performances and for comparing one group of athletes with another.

Sports facilities use computers to handle the two factors that have the most impact on their bottom line: inventory and scheduling. By managing inventory precisely, facilities can cut down on waste, eliminate long-term warehousing, and schedule payments to maximize cash-flow benefits. Scheduling is equally important. By having raw data available at their fingertips, managers are able to more accurately anticipate crowd sizes and to schedule their manpower needs accordingly.

Colleges use computers extensively, both to manage their recruiting efforts and to produce much of their public relations material via desktop publishing.

In addition, many sports use computers and computer systems for scoring events. Auto racers use computers extensively; they even have them on their cars, with monitors able to evaluate information about fuel consumption, engine performance, and system failures.

All in all, it is clear that as the sophistication and popularity of computer systems in sports increases, so will the need for better programmers and operators.

Getting a computer job in sports starts with building an expertise in computer systems and software. It pays to be something of a generalist in the area, as capable of putting together a linked computer system as you are of writing programs to solve a specific need in the ticketing department. Once you have built up this expertise, one way to get started is to volunteer to work for a major onetime or annual event in the area. Organizers could never afford to hire a computer specialist for these kinds of events, but they often need one to help them adapt their existing hardware to the event, choose software programs, train part-time help, and design scoring systems. By working with the promoter or manager of the event and becoming his or her computer expert, you may be able to get some experience in sports and start developing a reputation.

WHERE THE JOBS ARE: Metropolitan areas, colleges.

KEYS TO GETTING THE JOB:
• Expertise in computer systems, operations, and programs.
• Ability to expand capabilities of existing systems.

CORPORATE SPONSORSHIP

POSITION: Corporate sponsorship sales

EDUCATION/TRAINING: College degree usually required.

SALARY: Intro: $12,000
Average: $40,000
Top level: $125,000 plus

JOB DESCRIPTION: Professional and collegiate sports today depend on money from corporate sponsorships to survive. Because of the escalating costs of sports, even at the college level, few events can turn a profit with the proceeds from ticket sales. They all need revenue from other sources to make up the difference. More and more, this source is corporate sponsorships.

Whether it is paying for commercials on a television broadcast or paying a fee to be the sponsor of a sport or event, corporations are the key to the business of sports. Without companies willing to advertise their products, televised sports would be a thing of the past, as would sports on radio. The ability of a team, a league, a facility, a sports organization, or an event to attract corporate sponsors will often spell the difference between success and failure.

In a nutshell, corporate sponsorship sales is the job of attracting and managing corporate sponsorships. It includes making the sales pitch, insuring that all the elements of the agreement are adhered to, and managing all the fine points of the agreement. This includes such things as making sure that the correct commercial runs at the correct time, that the sponsor's sign is in the right place, that promotions run efficiently, that tickets are distributed, that hospitality arrangements for customers are made, and in general that the sponsor feels it is getting its money's worth.

Today, few companies are involved in sports for reasons of vanity or because they feel that as good corporate citizens they should support the local college team. Money is tight, and if it doesn't make good business sense, they won't do it.

Virtually every organization in sports today has a person or a staff of people devoted to helping corporations find ways to make the sponsorship of their sport a good idea. Getting one of these jobs usually starts by earning a degree in business or sports administration, followed by some experience in marketing or sales.

A sample career pathway in this field is that of John Cordova, who heads corporate sponsorship sales for the Milwaukee Brewers.

John graduated from college with the idea that he wanted to go into football coaching. After serving as a graduate assistant coach for a couple of years at New Mexico State, he decided that while he enjoyed the business of sports, coaching was not for him. So, he entered graduate school, earning an MBA. After graduate school, he was accepted to serve a paid internship with Major League Baseball's Executive Development Program in New York. It was during this internship that he began working with corporate sponsors. He found that he enjoyed this part of the business, and when his internship concluded he looked for jobs with major sports sponsors. He found one in the sports marketing department of the Miller Brewing Company. While with Miller, John continued to develop programs with Major League Baseball, and also worked with the USFL, the NFL, and the NBA. At Miller, he refined his knowledge of the kinds of things companies like to do and what works in the area of corporate sponsorships. After a few years, John made the jump back to corporate sales on the team side, as director of corporate marketing for the Brewers.

This kind of experience is common in the area of corporate sponsorships. The first step is to develop a strong educational background. After that, you need to become familiar both with the business of sports and the business of business; that is, how companies can use sponsorships to reach their corporate goals. You can either start on the sports side, helping teams and events solicit corporate sponsors, or on the business side, getting a job with a company that is involved in sports sponsorships and learning how they help the business. Once you know how and why they work, you will be ready to get a job selling sports sponsorships.

WHERE THE JOBS ARE: Teams, amateur and professional sports organizations, racing groups, media, facilities, colleges.

KEYS TO GETTING THE JOB:
• Good educational background.
• Broad knowledge of different types of businesses.
• Ability to develop creative solutions to business problems using sports.
• Familiarity with the business community.

POSITION: Corporate sponsorship administration

EDUCATION/TRAINING: College degree; MBA sometimes required.

SALARY: Intro: $15,000
Average: $40,000
Top level: $300,000 plus

JOB DESCRIPTION: As more and more companies and industries get involved in sports advertising and marketing, many of them are putting sports specialists on staff. These people decide which sports the company should sponsor, how much to spend, and how to best use the sponsorship, and they manage the promotional and sales programs built around sports.

For example, Bob's Sportswear, Inc., decides to spend ten million dollars in sports to build its image among men and to boost sales. The sports specialists have a lot of decisions to make. They are certainly going to spend money on sponsorships; the question is, which ones? The Super Bowl, the World Series, the Indianapolis 500, the Olympic Games? And how should the sponsorship be structured? These and other questions are handled by the corporate sponsorship administrator.

The job involves planning, budgeting, coordinating the actions of a few different departments of the company, and overall attention to detail and creativity.

Getting a job as a corporate sponsorship manager takes experience in media sponsorships and promotions. This kind of experience can be obtained by working at a radio station, for a nonprofit organization, a grocery store chain, a razor blade company—any group or company that promotes to consumers. Once you have some experience in the area of sponsorships and promotions, you will be able to tailor it to sports sponsorships.

WHERE THE JOBS ARE: Corporate headquarters and regional offices.

KEYS TO GETTING THE JOB:
• Understanding how to structure a promotion.
• Familiarity with media.
• Creativity in using sports to sell products or services.

CUSTOMER RELATIONS

POSITION: Customer relations director

EDUCATION/TRAINING: College degree, usually in liberal arts.

SALARY: Intro: $15,000
Average: $30,000
Top level: $55,000

JOB DESCRIPTION: Most professional teams and many sports facilities have on staff a customer relations director. This person acts as a liaison between the general public and the team or facility. The customer relations director gives the fan a direct line of communication to the team and provides the fan with much-needed information.

The customer relations director is primarily responsible for managing the public's concerns and questions on game days. This is usually accomplished by establishing information centers at the facility, run by a community relations staff. From this center, the community relations director handles any and all problems and inquiries.

A typical day may include dozens of requests for tickets (direct to ticket office or distribute ticket literature), first aid problems (call facility medical staff), or lost children (make announcement, serve ice cream); it may involve holding VIP building tours, taking job inquiries, distributing promotional giveaway items ("If you have the lucky number, go to the customer relations office on level three to claim your prize"), and handling the many and varied complaints of the fans, from the temperature of the hot dogs to the rudeness of the ushers. As the team or facility representative, you are up front and on the firing line. The good ones are worth their weight in gold, turning angry customers into satisfied customers who will return to buy tickets, T-shirts, pennants, and popcorn another day.

To get a job as a customer relations specialist, it is helpful to get some experience in working with the public. This can take many forms, from volunteering to man a booth at the county fair to working part-time giving guided tours of a facility. It is also very beneficial to know a great deal about the team, event, or facility you will be representing. Read its media guide, go to a series of events, and keep your eyes open. If you can demonstrate that you know the area well, and have experience under the fire of customer complaints, you will be ready for a job in sports customer relations.

WHERE THE JOBS ARE: Sports facilities; professional or college teams.

KEYS TO GETTING THE JOB:
• Experience in dealing with the public, especially in handling complaints.
• Thorough knowledge of the sport, team event, or facility.
• An outgoing personality and professional appearance.

DRIVER

POSITION: Driver

EDUCATION/TRAINING: Appropriate licenses and permits.

SALARY: Intro: $20,000
Average: $30,000
Top level: $50,000

JOB DESCRIPTION: There are some jobs in sports that consist of driving, besides driving race cars. For the most part, they consist of moving equipment or people from one part of the country to another.

Examples of sports jobs for drivers include driving buses for minor league baseball teams. Others are found in racing. Racing team owners need transport drivers to take their cars and equipment from one race to another. Some racing teams have private coaches that travel with them from race to race, to serve as a hospitality area at the racetrack. Many companies have show or display vehicles, identical replicas of real race cars, that are used for shopping malls, race course infields, and parking lots. These are moved around the country in large transporters, with the drivers serving as both driver, information guide, and merchandise salesman. Television networks and mobile television suppliers need drivers to get their mobile studios from the Twins game on Sunday to the Cardinals game on Thursday. The list goes on and on.

The job of the driver is simple, but the responsibility is large. People driving in the world of sports aren't carrying a load of potatoes; there's a couple of million dollars' worth of race car, or television equipment, or maybe even John Madden in the back.

The benefit is that once the trip has been made, the driver is usually free to enjoy the event. And for some reason, every driver in sports whom I have ever known really got to know a lot of the athletes and celebrities, and had a lot of fun most of the time. Maybe it's because drivers are the only people who are relaxed during events—their job doesn't start until the event is over. While everyone else is worried about qualifying times and getting enough commercial breaks in, the driver is just enjoying the game.

To get a driving job like this requires first and foremost a spotless driving record, coupled with the appropriate licenses to drive the kind of equipment you will have to drive. Beyond that, it requires doing your homework—identifying those companies or individuals that hire drivers and could use your help. In racing, this means going to a few races and talking with show-vehicle drivers, coach drivers, and transport drivers to see if there is someone you could talk with about a job. Unfortunately, this is not the kind of position that offers on-the-job training. If you are not qualified going in, you may as well not even try. But, if you don't mind a lot of travel and have a good record, your chances are about as good as anyone's.

WHERE THE JOBS ARE: Around the country with sports groups that need to travel or move a lot of equipment in order to compete. Minor league teams, small colleges, racers of every type.

KEYS TO GETTING THE JOB:
• Spotless driving record.
• Experience with the kind of equipment you will be driving.
• Ability to get along with a lot of different people.
• Strong sense of responsibility.
• Willingness to do lots of traveling and to be away from home most of the time.
• Professional appearance.

EDUCATION

POSITION: Sports administration professor

EDUCATION/TRAINING: Master's to begin teaching, Ph.D. to advance.

SALARY: Intro: $22,000
Average: $35,000
Top level: $65,000

JOB DESCRIPTION: There are currently over 170 public and private higher education institutions offering some kind of undergraduate or graduate degree program in sports administration. These programs may stand on their own or be a part of another department such as physical education or business. The job of teaching all of these classes goes to the sports administration professor.

Teaching classes in sports is a relatively new field. Over the last ten years, the number of colleges offering programs has exploded. Finding qualified people to teach in these programs has been difficult.

The job of a college professor is twofold at most institutions: to teach, and to do research. In the field of sports, just about the entire responsibility falls on the teaching side of the ledger. The average sports administration professor is required to teach from two to four classes each quarter or semester. These classes usually fall within that professor's particular area of expertise, whether it is sports history, sports psychology, sports business, or something else.

A career as a college professor requires a great deal of educational background to start. Most institutions can be very deliberate and are very careful about who they hire. But the environment around a college campus is unique, and very special to those who work there. Helping shape the minds of the leaders of tomorrow can be very rewarding for the sports administration professional.

Getting a job as a sports administration professor is not any different from getting a job in the English department. Openings are announced in various journals and at conventions, or may be uncovered by writing to the deans of the institutions that have sports administration or sports business departments.

WHERE THE JOBS ARE: Colleges and universities around the country.

KEYS TO GETTING THE JOB:
• Master's degree to start, Ph.D. soon after to advance.
• Desire to teach in a college setting.

ENGINEERING

POSITION: Sports engineer

EDUCATION/TRAINING: Degree in engineering, with specialization. Licensed state by state.

SALARY: Intro: $32,000
Average: $50,000
Top level: $150,000

JOB DESCRIPTION: Engineers design and build things. In sports, their skills are used in many areas, from the construction of major league stadiums to building a better golf club.

Engineering has become a very specialized field. A typical Yellow Pages directory will list fifty or more different kinds of engineering specialties, with more and more categories being defined all the time.

Just as there are many kinds of engineering, so are there many kinds of jobs available for engineers in sports. Here are some examples of the ways training and experience in selected engineering disciplines can develop into a job in sports:

ACOUSTICAL/SOUND ENGINEERS: These are the people who work to maximize the sound quality in a building. They work with teams, facilities, or engineering firms to design public-address and music systems for sports arenas and stadiums.

BROADCAST ENGINEERS: They design and maintain radio and television broadcasting systems. Sports jobs include working with stations that broadcast sports, radio and television sports networks, professional and amateur leagues, teams and facilities on broadcast-signal generation, transmission, and receiving.

CIVIL ENGINEERS: These are the engineers who work in facility construction, design race tracks, build access roadways, design golf course layouts, and so on.

COMMUNICATIONS ENGINEERS: They design, install, and maintain telephone and communication systems within sports facilities, in the press box area especially. They also work to connect the facilities to outside providers and subscribers.

ELECTRICAL ENGINEERS: More and more electrical engineers are working on sports-related projects. These include designing electrical systems for facilities and developing improved scoreboard systems, giant television screens, and replay systems.

GEOTECHNICAL ENGINEERS: These are the experts in soil composition, which is crucial in the areas of horse and dog racing track surface management, playing field soil composition studies, and the design of new and better natural turf fields.

LANDSCAPE ENGINEERS: Anywhere you find a sports facility, you will find the work of an engineer who has designed the landscape around it. These engineers are especially active in golf course design, in sports facility landscaping projects, and in park and recreation area layouts.

MECHANICAL ENGINEERS: Mechanical engineers build machines. The different kinds of sports machines they build include exercise equipment, race car chassis, and racing engines, to name a few.

STRUCTURAL ENGINEERS: Structural engineers build the buildings of sports, including arenas, stadiums, swimming pools, gymnasiums, and bowling alleys.

TRAFFIC ENGINEERS: They create systems to ease traffic congestion in and out of major facilities or special onetime events such as the Olympic Games, a golf tournament, or an auto race.

WHERE THE JOBS ARE: Engineering or architectural firms that specialize in sports projects; broadcast companies; telecommunications companies; major facilities; golf course design firms.

KEYS TO GETTING THE JOB:
• Strong educational background—top-notch performance at a good school.
• Interest in developing a specialty applicable to sports.
• Selecting the right situation. If you want to design sports facilities, don't join a firm that specializes in hydroelectric projects.

ENTERTAINMENT DIRECTOR

POSITION: Entertainment coordinator

EDUCATION/TRAINING: No specific requirements; college
degree preferred.

SALARY: Intro: $12,000
Average: $25,000
Top level: $50,000

JOB DESCRIPTION: As the competition for the entertainment dollar increases, the demands on a sports event to be more than just the
game also increase. Teams, sports, leagues, and facilities in the
nineties are trying to present an exciting package for the whole
family. They are striving to put on a show that includes nonstop
entertainment, taking advantage of any major breaks in their
events—before the game, between innings, between heats, during
time-outs, between periods, at halftime, and after the game. These
gaps are given to the entertainment coordinator to fill.

Virtually all of the nonsports elements of an event are handled by
the entertainment coordinator. For example, almost every sporting
contest starts with the national anthem. It is the job of the entertainment coordinator to see that someone is there each game to perform
it. After the anthem, each game or event evolves differently. In
football and basketball, plans must be made for halftime entertainment. In hockey, it's between periods; in baseball, between innings.
Frisbee-catching dogs, hoop-shooting contests, fan field-goal kicks,
cheerleader routines, or marching bands make up a typical halftime
entertainment. The Famous Chicken has made an entire career of
filling these breaks with his skits and clever antics.

Overall, the job consists of finding out what entertainment options
are available, managing their costs, and scheduling them at the

appropriate times. It is a little bit like booking acts into the largest lounge in the country. The acts must be in good taste and must enhance the product on the field without overshadowing it. If your team's performance isn't exactly championship calibre, you at least have shown the fans a good time before the game and during time-outs. They leave happy, and will come back again.

Surprisingly, the job of entertainment coordinator is often looked upon as an entry-level position. This is primarily due to the fact that the budget for the area is small or nonexistent. If you can't find people who are willing to perform for the glory of it and a pair of tickets, you are generally out of luck. Getting a job as entertainment coordinator requires being able to demonstrate a familiarity with the entertainment business, good organizational skills, and the ability to overcome adversity to get the job done. (If your anthem singer gets stuck in the snow, you'd better have a contingency plan.) A good way to get experience in this area is to work with your college or university in planning and executing halftime programs for its teams.

WHERE THE JOBS ARE: Major league baseball teams; NFL, NBA, and NHL teams; rodeos; some racing facilities; college athletics.

KEYS TO GETTING THE JOB:
• Contacts with a wide variety of performers and entertainers.
• Good head for details.
• Ability to come up with creative entertainment ideas that cost little or no money.

EQUIPMENT MANAGER

POSITION: Equipment manager

EDUCATION/TRAINING: No specific background required.

SALARY: Intro: $15,000
                Average: $35,000
                Top level: $150,000 plus (with bonus)

JOB DESCRIPTION: Today's athlete requires a great deal of equipment in order to compete. The job of making sure all of this equipment arrives where it is supposed to, on time, clean, and in good working shape, falls to the equipment manager.

A good equipment manager has to be a jack-of-all-trades. He must be able to organize the movement of many tons of equipment from city to city. He must be able to maintain and fix that equipment. And on top of that, he must be able to look after the individual needs of the players.

The job of the equipment manager starts in the locker room. This is his domain. He makes sure the players have everything they need there, from tape for their ankles to a good selection of snacks. He must order all the supplies, make sure the equipment that comes is right, manage all of the inventory, work with the trainers and team medical specialists to insure they have what they need, and cater to the individual needs of the athletes.

The second and toughest part of the equipment manager's job takes place on the road. He travels to all the games, just like the team does. He has to make sure each player's gear arrives at the hotel, or arena, or stadium. He has to plan to have enough tape, enough hockey sticks, enough spare helmet parts, no matter how long the road trip. He is responsible more than anyone else for the appearance of the team on the field, cleaning the players' uniforms, shining their shoes, even stitching their names on their uniforms.

The rewards for all this hard work are many. Equipment managers always become a real part of the team. They spend more time with the players during the season than the players' families do. When a team has some success, the equipment manager feels a part of it. And financially, equipment managers on successful teams do very well. It is common for them to receive a full World Series or Super Bowl share from the fund controlled by the players, a share that can amount to over $100,000.

Getting a job as equipment manager historically has not been the result of a long college degree program. However, today most managers do get their start in college, working with the equipment for their college teams. Once they have their degree, they start with a football team as an assistant equipment manager, or work at a training camp, or start working with a minor league baseball or hockey team. This gives them a chance to add to their knowledge about the equipment needed for that particular sport, and gives them some experience in dealing with players. It is then a matter of keeping their eyes open for opportunities.

WHERE THE JOBS ARE: Professional teams and colleges in the U.S. and Canada.

KEYS TO GETTING THE JOB:
• Ability to form a good relationship with players.
• Willingness to do any "dirty work" that needs to be done.
• Familiarity with equipment, plus the know-how to maintain and repair it if necessary.

FACILITY MANAGEMENT

POSITION: Facility management

EDUCATION/TRAINING: College degree in sports administration, business, or management; master's degree preferred.

SALARY: Intro: $20,000
Average: $35,000
Top level: $150,000

JOB DESCRIPTION: Sports facility management has been one of the major growth areas in sports over the past twenty years. The construction of large, multipurpose facilities like the Superdome, the Silverdome, and the Meadowlands complex created the need for large staffs of professionals in a wide variety of fields to manage them.

Sports facilities come in all shapes and sizes. Most communities host sporting events of some sort or another, whether it is the rodeo at the fairgrounds or the holiday high school basketball tournament at the community center. The frequency and scope of these events determine the need for a full-time sports and event administrator. On the other end of the scale, stadiums, arenas, racetracks, and other spectator-sports venues may employ hundreds of people, both full- and part-time, who work around the clock to keep up with the variety of events they attract.

In many ways, a large sports facility is just like any other large building, with many of the same job opportunities. The building has to be maintained, its heating and cooling systems need to be cared for, it has to be cleaned, it has to have security, and general repairs and remodeling have to be done periodically. All of these functions exist in sports facilities as well, presenting opportunities for those who want to take advantage of them.

There are, however, some jobs with sports facilities that are more unique, that are more closely tied with the business of sports. It is these jobs we will be describing.

It is important to note that many facilities used for sports have been funded and are controlled, at least in part, by government entities, such as the city or the county. The application and hiring processes for jobs at these facilities are very similar to those for any other government position. The job openings are posted and advertised well in advance, and anyone who meets the minimum qualifications is encouraged to apply. This often makes the hiring process more equitable. On the other hand, it can slow down the selection process considerably and dramatically increase the pool of applicants, leading to more competition for jobs. But in the end, working for facilities under public control can lead to greater job security and even better salaries and benefits than working for some private facilities, especially at lower- and middle-management levels. For senior and top managers, however, private facilities will almost always have better compensation packages than public ones, mainly because they can be more creative and generous when tying compensation in with performance.

Major facilities can have as many as a thousand people or more working on a part-time basis, including ushers, security people, ticket sellers, parking attendants, cleanup people, concession sales people, and event-specific staff members. The size of the full-time management staff is much smaller, and by the time you get to mid-level or senior management positions the numbers shrink even more. Nevertheless, these are the positions that allow you the closest association with sports, the kinds of jobs that make an excellent and rewarding career.

The following are some brief job descriptions of jobs available in facilities management:

ADMINISTRATION: Manage full- and part-time staff; handle personnel processing and scheduling; order and store supplies; do inventory; oversee clerical staff.

EVENT MANAGEMENT: At most facilities, every event is assigned to an event manager. This manager acts as the liaison between the facility and the promoter, team, or event producer. He or she serves as an information and resource person, helping the event come off as smoothly and productively as possible. This job often requires being able to come up with creative solutions to problems with equipment, scheduling, staffing, and so on. To get an event management job at a major facility requires experience at smaller facilities.

FIELD MAINTENANCE: A specialized part of the overall maintenance program. In this category are grouped the groundskeepers, the people who manage the installation and movement of artificial turf, and racetrack surface managers. Expertise in soil and turf engineering is a plus. At facilities with artificial turf, expertise in cleaning, maintenance, and repair are essential.

FINANCE: Manage administrative financial matters such as payroll, retirement, and taxes. Oversee payment/collection of revenue to owner or government body; manage funds, financial liaison with tenants, and contract negotiations.

FOOD SERVICE: Manage concessions or work with contracted outside concessionaire. Safeguard food quality, monitor costs, supervise part-time sales staff, develop special catering and hospitality programs. Negotiate contracts with suppliers, manage the food supply to minimize warehousing and waste and maximize quality and profits.

MAINTENANCE/OPERATIONS: Manage full- and part-time staff members responsible for facility, including operation of the physical plant, heating, cooling, and lighting. Supervise most of the part-time staff, including janitors, security personnel, parking attendants, ushers, electricians, plumbers, and other maintenance people. Responsible for scheduling, budgeting.

MANAGEMENT: This refers to very senior-level positions, including the president or executive director. Manage facility budgets. Act as liaison between facility and key tenants. Manage administrative staff. Accountable for facility profitability. Often report to government entity, such as sports authority, city council, board of supervisors, or mayor's office. Raise funds for facility updates and improvements. Set long-term policy and direction for facility.

MARKETING: Prepare and execute plans to increase use of facility. Direct advertising campaigns. Generate revenue through corporate sponsorships. Help tenants market their events. Develop programs to attract new clients. Supervise special events.

PUBLIC RELATIONS: Manage facility publicity, working with local, regional, and national media outlets. Act as community relations director, working with outside organizations on special uses of the building. Produce print materials relating to facility, from maps and brochures to press releases. Work with tenants to generate stories on upcoming events.

SALES: Sales jobs at a facility can take a variety of forms. They can include inside sales positions, such as managing food and beverages, souvenir merchandise, and ticket sales. They can involve being responsible for generating revenue from sponsorship or advertising sales, such as by selling signs in a stadium or commercial announcements on a replay screen in an arena. Or they can entail selling the facility itself, seeking clients who want to lease the facility on a daily, weekly, or seasonal basis. Sales is such an important part of the success of a facility that senior management is almost always involved in some capacity.

TECHNICAL DIRECTOR: Manage audiovisual capability, scoreboard, large-screen television, in-house studio production; liaison with television and radio personnel.

WHERE THE JOBS ARE: Medium to large cities across the country; college campus facilities.

KEYS TO GETTING THE JOB:

• Educational background in sports management, business. Master's degree preferred.
• Some experience in facility management. Get it by serving internships while in school or working at one of the many part-time positions available.

FINANCE

POSITION: Financial management

EDUCATION/TRAINING: College degree in business, accounting, or related field. Completion of CPA exam often required. MBA degree preferred.

SALARY: Intro: $20,000
Average: $35,000
Top level: $150,000

JOB DESCRIPTION: Every sports organization has at least one person on staff who is responsible for the business end of the operation. This is the person who makes sure all revenue is accounted for, the bills paid, tax deadlines and payroll met, and the cash flow properly managed.

These jobs in sports finance have a wide variety of titles and job descriptions. Small organizations have one person who does it all, while a major league team may have a financial staff of a dozen people or more.

What follows is a list of the most common jobs in sports finance. These may be combined in many different ways to form the job you are actually after. (For example, one person may handle both payroll and accounts payable.) You should do some research on the company you are interested in joining to see how it divides these financial responsibilities.

ACCOUNTS PAYABLE: This job, in the most simplistic terms, is paying the bills for the organization. It is identifying what the company owes and writing the checks to cover the debt. This job becomes very important in managing the flow of cash through the organization. Paying accounts exactly when they are due means the company gets to hold onto revenue as long as possible. During the time gap between billing and payment, it can therefore keep this revenue working for it in investment vehicles, earning interest. Paying accounts early defeats this strategy, while paying them late can result in fines or ultimately the loss of credit. It's the accounts payable clerk's job to make sure neither of these things happen. This job is often combined with accounts receivable.

ACCOUNTS RECEIVABLE: The accounts receivable clerk is the person responsible for handling billing and collection of revenue, making sure that cash is flowing into the organization in a timely manner. This often means qualifying suppliers' ability to pay, doing background financial checks, managing the billing process, and, in the worst cases, handling collection of debts owed the company. This job is often combined with accounts payable.

AUDITING: Audits of sports organizations are done by outside organizations, usually medium to large accounting firms. There are within these accounting firms some people who specialize in sports audits. They may work with a facility every year, for example, preparing the financial statement for its annual report. Outside audits are done to insure that the team, facility, organization, or group is reporting its financial status accurately. The auditor works with the sports organization's financial staff in preparing the required documents.

CONTRACT MANAGEMENT: As the amount of money involved in the business of sports has increased, it has become more and more important to have a person or people on board who can help manage contracts. For professional teams, this means making sure athletes are paid on time, annuities are set up, scholarship programs are established, incentive bonuses are paid, and all of the other stipulations in the various contracts are adhered to. For corporations, it means making sure all of the requirements of every contract are met, even though the people who signed the contract may have long since left the company. Contract managers also can play a part in the negotiation of contracts. For example, in the NBA, before a prize rookie can be offered a large amount of money the team has to make sure it will fit under the salary cap.

CONTROLLER: Most medium to large sports organizations have a controller. This is the person who oversees the financial operation, making sure the accounting staff is doing their job and that there is enough cash available to do the things they need to do in both the short and long term, and in general managing the flow of cash for the organization. If a sports company has only one person in its financial department, chances are very good that person will have the title of controller.

FINANCIAL PLANNING: The role of the financial planner is increasing every year in sports. This is the person who helps the individual athlete or sports administrator manage his or her money. He may work for a sports marketing firm like IMG or for a financial planning firm that specializes in sports, or may be under contract to a team or facility. He is often on his own, managing his own business. With the millions of dollars being paid to people in sports every year come stories of athletes blowing it all and ending up broke, or of broadcasters getting into an investment scheme that ended up being a scam, or of high-level administrators working all their life and, at the end of it all, having nothing for retirement. The financial planner has stepped into the sports field to help prevent these kinds of problems, working with the people in sports to develop sound investment strategies that will insure that their personal financial goals are met for the rest of their lives.

INSURANCE: Insurance is a big part of sports in the nineties. College athletes take out insurance policies before their senior year to make sure they are taken care of in case of injury. Facilities have to pay large premiums for liability coverage in case an accident happens during an event. They can even buy insurance against someone making a basket from half-court during a halftime basketball contest. If he misses, they are only out the premium payment: if he makes it, the insurance company buys him the new car. With all the lawsuits flying back and forth and the money invested in things as fragile as a pitcher's arm or a horse's legs, insurance has become as important as any other financial tool in sports. Many an event has been canceled because adequate insurance could not be obtained. More and more, organizations are hiring insurance specialists to assist them in managing all of the different policies they are required to have, keeping premiums down, and working with insurance companies on claims.

INVESTMENT MANAGEMENT: Sports organizations generate a good deal of cash. Major events can have gate receipts well into the millions of dollars. It is the job of the investment manager to put this money to work. For example, an NFL team may receive a hundred-dollar deposit from each of its 50,000 season-ticket holders six months before the start of the next season. That's five million dollars. The team won't have to start spending that money until the season begins, so it invests it in six-month notes that return eight percent annually. That season-ticket deposit money thus earns the team two hundred thousand dollars—enough to pay for five or six front office employees for the year. Investment managers are constantly studying different investment options, weighing their return against the risk involved, deciding how long they can afford to keep the cash tied up, and planning for future expenditures. It is a complex balancing act, but one that pays great dividends for the sports organization.

PAYROLL: Ask those in any organization who their favorite co-worker is, and chances are they will point to the person who gives them their paycheck every two weeks. In small sports companies, the payroll clerk also wears other hats. But in the larger organizations, keeping track of payroll, vacations, sick leave, bonuses, severance, and all of the various tax and payroll deductions can be a very daunting task. The payroll administrator is the person who looks after all of these details.

TAXES: All companies have to pay taxes. But in many cases, sports organizations are required to keep even closer tabs on their tax liability, and to make even more frequent reports to local, state, and federal tax organizations. Sales tax, income tax, payroll taxes, and property taxes can be and are supplemented by admissions taxes, entertainment taxes, and use taxes. Sports such as horse and dog racing are required to pay especially close attention to their daily tax situation. It is therefore very helpful for sports organizations to have a tax specialist on hand, both to monitor the collection and payment of taxes and to insure that no under- or overpayments take place. The job requires a lot of interaction with government agencies and a thorough knowledge of the various tax codes and regulations.

WHERE THE JOBS ARE: Jobs in finance can be found in any sports organization, including leagues, teams, events, promotion companies, facilities, and manufacturers.

KEYS TO GETTING THE JOB:
• Strong educational background, usually consisting of a college degree in business, finance, or accounting. MBAs and CPAs are getting most of the top positions.
• Familiarity with the sport.
• Good head for details.
• Expertise in a particular area, such as taxes or personal finance.

FOOD SERVICE

POSITION: Caterer

EDUCATION/TRAINING: Degree in food service, restaurant management.

SALARY: Intro: $15,000
Average: $25,000
Top level: $100,000

JOB DESCRIPTION: Sports caterers fall into two categories: those who work for concessionaires and those who work for independent catering companies.

All large sports concessionaires—the people who manage the concession stands at stadiums and arenas—have the ability to do some catering. Most have a catering department, whose responsibility includes all of the special catering needs of their sports clients.

Independent caterers run their own business, contracting with sports teams, facilities, organizations, promoters, and even athletes to meet their special food service needs.

The job of the caterer is to work with the client on single-event meal services. Regular caterers do this in office buildings or in hotels. Sports caterers do it at the Super Bowl, or during the Final Four.

These single events may string together to form a series, but they are still treated individually. For example, a caterer may be asked to provide an evening meal service for the corporate marketing suite at every home baseball game. That covers eighty-one separate dates. Each night's menu is a little bit different, to offer the people who are there every night a little bit of variety. Or, a caterer may be asked to provide meals to a racing team's hospitality tent, three meals a day for five days. But each one should be a little bit different.

Caterers are used a great deal in the area of corporate hospitality. From beside a sand trap at a golf tournament to atop a snow-covered mountainside for a ski race, caterers specialize in providing high-quality food and beverage service in difficult situations. They charge a premium for this, of course, but companies are more than willing to pay for quality.

Independent caterers run the most risk, but have the greatest chance to make the most money in the food service business. Much of a caterer's success comes from word-of-mouth advertising and a good reputation. By being dependable, serving high-quality food, hiring competent part-time help, and being a little bit creative with food preparation and presentation, a single caterer can take over virtually all of the sports business in his market area. And barring any disasters, chances are good he will keep that business for a long time.

Getting a job as a caterer requires a solid foundation in the area of food service. This can be obtained through one of the excellent college programs in the field or by working in the business for a number of years at a lower level. Caterers, especially ones that do large sporting events, are always looking for strong part-time help. Moving up the ladder requires the ability to adjust food and labor costs to maximize profits, being able to attract clients, and having some creativity and imagination when it comes to menu development and problem solving. The next thing you know, you will be working with NBC Sports, deciding what to serve its network affiliates at the Super Bowl party.

WHERE THE JOBS ARE: With concessionaires, catering companies, racetracks, leagues, and sports organizations.

KEYS TO GETTING THE JOB:
• Educational background.
• Experience in food service.
• Dependability.
• Creativity.
• Ability to work with deadlines and strict budgets.

POSITION: Concessionaire

EDUCATION/TRAINING: College degree in business, food and restaurant management.

SALARY: Intro: $20,000
Average: $35,000
Top level: $100,000

JOB DESCRIPTION: There are many companies across the country that specialize in food service at sports facilities, arenas, and stadiums. A dozen or so of them are very large, with contracts to handle the food service operations of the major facilities across the country. These include companies like Ogden Allied, ARA, Sports Service, Canteen, Volume Service, Marriott, and Harry M. Stevens.

The job of concessionaires is to sell spectators food and beverages. They give the facility, the promoter, or the teams a percentage of the earnings and keep the rest. They hire all of the staff needed to do the job, take care of all of the equipment and special supplies, and make all of the capital investments necessary to maximize the amount of revenue generated by concession sales. In return, they receive long-term exclusive contracts.

Most of the people working in concessions are part-time employees. The full-time management staff usually numbers between ten and thirty people, depending on the size of the facility. Responsibilities include working with the labor force, scheduling, hiring, working with suppliers, managing the catering operation, overseeing food development, and working with the clients. The secret to success in the business is careful planning and management of people and inventory. You need to make sure you have enough people to work the concession stands, but not so many that they stand around idly. You need to be sure you have enough popcorn for a weekend baseball home stand, but not so much that you waste a lot of it when the team leaves town for two weeks.

Getting a job in food service at a sports facility is relatively easy, in that it is fairly simple to get experience in the field. In general, food service at Madison Square Garden is not very different from food service at a hotel, a school, or a hospital. Therefore, any related experience you can get can be applied to sports-facility food service. Plus, facilities have almost constant openings for part-time help, which is another way to get started in the business.

WHERE THE JOBS ARE: Stadiums, arenas, racetracks, and other sports facilities.

KEYS TO GETTING THE JOB:
• Educational background.
• Some food service experience.

HALL OF FAME/MUSEUMS

POSITION: Hall of Fame/museum administration

EDUCATION/TRAINING: College degree in sports administration, museumology.

SALARY: Intro: $15,000
Average: $30,000
Top level: $60,000

JOB DESCRIPTION: Museums that feature sports memorabilia usually fall under the description of a sports Hall of Fame. These museums are sport-specific; that is, they feature artifacts, memorabilia, and photographs of one particular sport, from its beginning until the present day.

The most prominent Halls of Fame are the ones that feature collections from the most popular sports, such as the Baseball Hall of Fame in Cooperstown, New York; the Pro Football Hall of Fame in Canton, Ohio; and the Hockey Hall of Fame in Toronto, Canada. But there are at least forty other sports Halls of Fame, including ones for figure skating, golf, fishing, and horse racing. To fans of these sports, these museums are very important.

The mission of any sports museum is to research the history of the sport from its earliest days, to preserve the items that reflect that history, to honor specific individuals and performances that have contributed to the sport, and ultimately to entertain. In its mission, a sports Hall of Fame is no different from the Louvre or the Metropolitan Museum of Art.

Halls of Fame are almost exclusively charitable, nonprofit organizations. They exist by charging admission to the public to see the exhibits, by attracting charitable contributions, and sometimes by soliciting subsidies from professional leagues or individuals. Because of their nonprofit status, salaries and benefits in these jobs are somewhat lower than the industry average.

Jobs at sports museums generally break down into seven areas: acquisitions, administration, exhibit coordination, finance, marketing, public relations, and research. Descriptions of these are as follows:

ACQUISITIONS: Locate and negotiate fees for purchase of items to be preserved and put on display in the museum. A great deal of time is spent talking with collectors and tracing the families of former athletes and coaches to find photographs, letters, or other personal items to add to the collection.

ADMINISTRATION: Manage the museum and staff; handle personnel, clerical staff, scheduling. Work with the museum board of directors on setting and meeting the annual budget, doing capital improvements, and sustaining fund-raising projects. Interface with leagues, teams, coaches, players, and supporters of the sport.

EXHIBIT COORDINATION: Decide what part of the collection should go on display and how it should be displayed. Design and build display areas. This job calls for a great deal of creativity.

FINANCE: General financial administration, including accounting, payroll, accounts receivable and payable, tax management, and asset management. Nonprofit nature of museums requires some specialized training in that area.

MARKETING: Help create interest in the museum and build attendance through radio, television, and print advertising campaigns, manage use of direct mail, create and administer special events, build opportunities for companies to use the museum in cross-promotions, license the Hall of Fame name.

PUBLIC RELATIONS: Generate publicity for museum, highlight new exhibits and inductees, work with community and sport's sanctioning body to build interest in the history of the sport, work with media on stories about the history of the sport.

RESEARCH: Authenticate museum acquisitions, do research on the sport and its participants to provide background for museum exhibits, respond to questions from the media and public about the sport.

To get a job with a sports museum, a good place to begin is to work for it during its busy periods. For the most part, this is during the summer months when the number of visitors is high, or a few months before a special event like the Hall of Fame football game in Canton every July. Since they are seasonal in nature, these jobs have quite a bit of turnover and are easier to get than full-time positions. This gives the people at the Hall of Fame a chance to get to know you and see what you can do, and for you to see where you think you could fit into the organization.

WHERE THE JOBS ARE: Major museums in Canton, Cooperstown, Toronto, and Springfield, Massachusetts. Minor museums in cities across the U.S. and Canada.

KEYS TO GETTING THE JOB:
• Degree in sports administration or museumology.
• Thorough knowledge of the sport.
• Willingness to work for smaller compensation than in other sports professions.
• Getting a part-time or seasonal job, or an internship at a Hall of Fame.

HEALTH CARE

POSITION: Chiropractor

EDUCATION/TRAINING: Degree in chiropractic medicine required.

SALARY: Intro: $35,000
Average: $70,000
Top level: $150,000

JOB DESCRIPTION: Chiropractors manipulate the spine and other parts of the skeletal structure to relieve pressure on nerves, increase circulation in muscles, and relieve muscular—especially back—pain. Athletes are either referred to a chiropractor by a team physician or go on their own.

While still not fully integrated into some parts of the medical community, chiropractic medicine has proven to be an effective treatment for a variety of complaints. Many athletes can testify to the benefits they received from chiropractors, which is all the endorsement needed to build a good client base in the area of sports medicine.

To become a chiropractor, one must attend a chiropractic medical school. There, you are taught the philosophy and techniques used in the profession. After graduation, you may join a clinic or start one on your own, with a specialty in sports-related injury treatment.

WHERE THE JOBS ARE: Clinics that receive referrals from professional sports teams; individual athletes; colleges.

KEYS TO GETTING THE JOB:
• Educational background.
• Particular expertise in kinds of treatments required by competitive athletes.

POSITION: Dentist

EDUCATION/TRAINING: DDS required.

SALARY: Intro: $50,000
                 Average: $80,000
                 Top level: $250,000

JOB DESCRIPTION: Dentists are not as closely affiliated with sports as are other medical professions. Dental problems are much rarer than other kinds of injuries, except in contact sports like hockey and football. Nevertheless, most professional sports teams and organizations have set up relationships with dentists to take care of their athletes.

Becoming a dentist requires a degree from an accredited dental school. If you are interested in sports dentistry, it is very helpful to emphasize the study of problems common to athletes while you are still in dental school, and to serve internships with sports dental specialists. This will not only prepare you for work with athletes, but will enable you to build a reputation as well.

Getting a job as a sports dentist, of course, requires the development of the kind of expertise needed in the sport you are interested in. Once that is accomplished, most dentists in the sports field sign contracts with particular teams, colleges, or facilities, agreeing to handle emergencies and to give the athletes and their families priority over other patients. The key ingredient is being able to work with the athletes at any time of the day or night, or on weekends. To get hired, the dentist must conform to the schedule of the athlete, and not restrict him or her to visits during office hours. For this, the dentist receives a retainer, a fee for services, and the ability to promote the fact that he or she is the dentist for the team.

WHERE THE JOBS ARE: Clinics serving professional sports teams, colleges, facilities, organizations, events.

KEYS TO GETTING THE JOB:
• Educational background.
• Willingness to put athletes ahead of other patients.
• High professional standing.

POSITION: Doctor

EDUCATION/TRAINING: MD required.

SALARY: Intro: $50,000
Average: $80,000
Top level: $250,000

JOB DESCRIPTION: The team doctor is as familiar a sight to most college and professional athletes as the head coach. Every college and professional team member or individual athlete needs professional medical help during his or her career. The lucky ones just go in for regular checkups, but most require help with injuries or illness. With salaries, prize money, and bonuses escalating so rapidly, athletes cannot afford to sit on the sidelines nursing an injury. The window of opportunity to win championships and earn money is very small, and they know it. That is why their doctor is so important to them.

Professional teams, leagues, organizations, and even facilities have relationships with doctors. These take one of two forms. Either the doctor is a permanent member of the staff, or he or she has a contractual arrangement with the team, facility, et al. to provide medical care when needed. The latter is by far the most prevalent arrangement.

The sports doctor is called upon to be present at sporting events in case of a problem, to treat injuries on site in an emergency situation if needed, to administer treatment and supervise therapy after an injury has occurred, and to conduct physical examinations and work with the rest of the training and medical team on conditioning, nutrition, and injury prevention. In today's sports environment, doctors also help manage the area of substance abuse, including misuse of recreational drugs and performance-enhancement drugs like steroids.

Becoming a sports doctor requires earning a degree from an accredited medical school, plus serving an internship and residency. If sports medicine is of particular interest, it is helpful to specialize in areas that are needed in the world of sports, such as orthopedics, internal medicine, surgery, and psychiatry, as opposed to such other choices as obstetrics or pediatrics. No matter how much you love sports or how high you finish in your class, if you trained as a pediatrician you will never get the chance to work with the Cincinnati Bengals.

Getting a job with a sports organization requires establishing a reputation in the field of sports medicine. This can be done through volunteer work on the high school or even the college level, or by specializing in a certain kind of procedure, or by publishing academic articles and achieving a level of recognition by your peers that can be used as a selling point. Unfortunately, given two doctors with equal credentials, it is still more often than not the one who "knows someone" in the sports organization who lands the position. However, because of the money involved and the complexity of the procedures taking place in the field, more and more top-quality doctors are getting jobs in sports based on their credentials and not on who their neighbor is.

As important as good standing in the medical community is the ability to give top-notch service to the team, facility, or athletes. This means being on call twenty-four hours a day during the season, traveling to all of the home and away games or events, giving preferential treatment to the athletes, and in short being there whenever and wherever you are needed. For this special attention, the doctor is compensated by being put on a retainer and then being paid an additional fee for services as they are rendered.

WHERE THE JOBS ARE: Teams, individual athletes, organizations, college athletics, events, facilities.

KEYS TO GETTING THE JOB:
• Educational background, with emphasis on sports medicine.
• Willingness to put athletes ahead of other patients.
• Availability around the clock.
• Ability to travel to competition site.

POSITION: Ophthalmologist

EDUCATION/TRAINING: Degree in ophthalmology required.

SALARY: Intro: $60,000
Average: $100,000
Top level: $200,000

JOB DESCRIPTION: An ophthalmologist is the person who takes care of the athlete's eyes. Most of the time, this means working with the athlete on such things as contact-lens fittings and glasses, but it can include treatment of eye injuries as well.

Most teams and athletic organizations have relationships with eye doctors. Again, the typical form this relationship takes is for the ophthalmologist to be under contract to provide care twenty-four hours a day, as needed. In return, the ophthalmologist is paid a retainer and fees for other services as rendered.

Just about every professional sport today requires excellent vision. Whether hitting a baseball thrown at ninety miles an hour, catching a football, or driving around a racetrack, athletes need to be able to see clearly. Working with the athletes to make sure their vision is sharp may not make the difference in whether or not they can participate in their sport, but it can dramatically affect their performance. For that reason, the ophthalmologist is an important member of the medical team.

Becoming a sports ophthalmologist requires expertise in vision correction and injury treatment. Beyond that, it requires a commitment to put the athlete's needs ahead of other patients', the willingness to work around the athlete's schedule, and having an interest in sports.

WHERE THE JOBS ARE: Teams, sports organizations, leagues, colleges, events.

KEYS TO GETTING THE JOB:
• Educational background.
• Willingness to put athletes ahead of other patients.
• Availability to handle emergencies and to travel if needed.

POSITION: Orthopedic surgeon

EDUCATION/TRAINING: MD required, with residency in
                   orthopedics.

SALARY: Intro: $100,000
                   Average: $250,000
                   Top level: $500,000

JOB DESCRIPTION: The orthopedic surgeon is the "miracle worker" of the modern sports medicine world. Careers such as that of baseball pitcher Orel Hershiser are extended because of the breakthrough work being done in the field of orthopedic surgery. In the sixties, a knee operation was a huge procedure, and most of the time meant an end to one's career. Now, players in college or even in high school talk about getting their knee "scoped" (undergoing arthroscopic surgery) with less anxiety than they would have about getting a tooth filled. An injury that would have crippled someone even a decade ago can now be repaired to allow the athlete to live a normal life, and in many cases to compete at a high level again.

Because orthopedics is a rapidly advancing part of sports medicine, it is necessary to get the best, most current training and experience you can in order to succeed in the field. This means doing your internship and residency in places that have good doctors you can learn from and that give you an opportunity to see a lot of different cases. For example, what better place to learn about knee injuries than near a large ski area? What a doctor in Texas or Florida might see once or twice a year is seen every day in places like Colorado and Utah. It is this kind of training and experience that will enable you to become a leader in the field, building the kind of reputation you need to work in the area of sports orthopedic surgery.

Once you have that experience, getting affiliated with a sports organization is a matter of reputation. For example, professional football teams work with doctors they "hear are good" from others in the profession or from athletes who have been treated successfully by them. They are also looking for those willing to sacrifice a bit of their practice to spend the kind of time and energy needed to work with professional athletes on a regular basis. Like others in this field, the usual kind of relationship is one of a retainer plus payment for services rendered.

Because of the ever changing nature of the field and the large amounts of money involved, the bottom line on sports orthopedic medicine is this: if you are good, and you know how to help athletes get better so they can perform again, you can write your own ticket.

WHERE THE JOBS ARE: Teams, facilities, sports organizations, events, clinics, hospitals.

KEYS TO GETTING THE JOB:
• Educational background.
• Expertise in sports-related injuries.
• Willingness to put athletes ahead of other patients
• Availability for events and to travel and be on call twenty-four hours a day, if necessary.

POSITION: Physical therapy

EDUCATION/TRAINING: Physical therapy degree required.

SALARY: Intro: $20,000
Average: $45,000
Top level: $150,000

JOB DESCRIPTION: The physical therapist is part of the medical injury treatment team. The therapist uses exercise techniques and equipment in partnership with a physician to help the injured athlete regain the strength and flexibility he or she may have lost due to injury. An example of a person who recently underwent extensive physical therapy was Indy car driver A. J. Foyt. Following a major crash in 1990, Foyt spent months in therapy working to regain the use of his legs and feet. The result was that in 1991 he was able to race again at the Indianapolis 500. In these situations, the television cameras capture the athlete walking on the treadmill and jumping on the trampoline. But what they don't show is the physical therapist who designed the rehab program, and who is also there pushing and prodding the athlete to make sure he or she is making a little progress each day.

Becoming a physical therapist in sports medicine requires a degree from an accredited physical therapy school, plus a license from the state in which you wish to work. Serving an internship in a clinic that specializes in sports medicine is a very important ingredient in starting your career in this area. Again, the key is exposure to a large number of injuries and patients with common sports injuries. Working on dozens and dozens of back and neck injuries will do you less good than getting the chance to work with ankles, knees, elbows, and shoulders, which are far and away the most common areas for sports injuries.

Physical therapists working in sports medicine typically are associated with hospitals or clinics or have their own independent practices. Few teams or other sports organizations have their own therapists on staff. They use therapists under referral from doctors, on a consulting basis. But, if a therapist develops a good relationship with a specific doctor, say the team doctor for the local NHL franchise, it usually results in a steady number of athlete referrals throughout the season.

WHERE THE JOBS ARE: Clinics, hospitals.

KEYS TO GETTING THE JOB:
• Educational background.
• Experience in treating sports-related injuries.

POSITION: Psychology

EDUCATION/TRAINING: Master's in psychology, counseling psychology, or sports psychology; Ph.D. preferred. For psychiatrists, MD required. Strong athletic background required.

SALARY: Intro: $20,000
Average: $100,000
Top level: $180,000

JOB DESCRIPTION: Sports psychologists and psychiatrists help athletes in two major ways: performance enhancement and problem solving.

In the area of performance enhancement, psychologists help the athlete improve concentration skills, enabling the golfer to make those six-foot putts under pressure or the tennis player to get his serve in when playing a player ranked in the top ten. They help the athlete visualize success, which makes it easier for him or her to achieve success. They also help the athlete cope with the frustrations of sports, such as dealing with the failure to live up to very lofty (and often unrealistic) expectations, or being patient with one's personal development schedule.

Other problems athletes may encounter may be more significant to them, but not a part of their sport per se—things such as marital problems, phobias, homesickness, weight problems, and financial difficulties. Psychiatrists are also helping more and more athletes deal with substance abuse, enabling them to get proper treatment.

As the money invested in athletes increases, more and more people are looking at keeping the mind of the athlete as sharp and as focused as the body. The psychologist and psychiatrist help with that process.

WHERE THE JOBS ARE: Teams, leagues, individual athletes.

KEYS TO GETTING THE JOB:
• Educational background, with master's degree, MD, or Ph.D.
• Sports background, including a familiarity with the athletes and the game. A sports psychologist may have great academic training, but if he doesn't know a curveball from a slider a baseball player will never trust him.

HORSE RACING

Racing, including thoroughbred horses, quarter horses, harness racing, and greyhound racing, is a unique sporting industry in a couple of important ways. Foremost of these is the fact that wagering is a big part of the racing experience. Handicapping and betting are as much a part of these sports as is the competition between the athletes.

Because wagering is involved in these sports, they are all regulated at the state level. This means that the industry is regulated by a state commission, appointed by the governor, and that the state imposes a direct tax on the business, over and above any sales taxes. For the job hunter, this means that work is available not only at the racing facility, but at the state level as well.

Racing jobs can be separated into two basic categories: administrative positions and racing positions. Administrative positions are those that deal with the business of running a racing facility. Most of these are similar to sports administration positions in other businesses. Racing positions are specific to that sport, are more technical in nature, and require an expertise in racing.

One way to get this expertise is to obtain a college degree in racetrack management, such as the one offered by the University of Arizona. Many of today's young racing administrators are graduates of programs such as this one.

Because racing is a seasonal business, most of the jobs in racing are seasonal as well. There are some full-time positions available, particularly top management and financial jobs, but the majority of employees will be paid on a contract basis for the season, or by the week, or even by the day or the hour. A general rule is that the larger the racing facility, the more full-time staff positions will be available.

To expand their seasonal jobs into something more full-time, many people work at different tracks at different times of the year. In Los Angeles, for example, when the racing season at Santa Anita is over, it is time for Hollywood Park and Del Mar to begin. By the time they are finished, it is time to get back to Santa Anita again. By becoming migratory and working at whichever facility is open at the time, even seasonal staff members can turn racing into a year-round occupation.

I have included the major management and racing positions and examples of some of the more unique seasonal positions at a typical horse racing facility. Smaller tracks will combine a number of these functions into one position, while the largest tracks may have as many as a dozen people working on just one of them. These positions are representative of the kinds of jobs available.

In terms of geography, racing positions are located where there are racing facilities. For the most part, this means major metropolitan areas, with more tracks in the Eastern part of the country than in the West.

Compensation in racing varies a great deal from track to track. The general rule of thumb is the larger the attendance and handle (total amount of money wagered in a day), the more money the track is able to pay its employees. Just as with other careers, jobs in major markets such as Los Angeles, New York, and Chicago tend to pay more than comparable positions in cities where the cost of living is lower.

POSITION: Agent, jockey

EDUCATION/TRAINING: No specific training required, but most jockey agents are former jockeys.

SALARY: Intro: $20,000
Average: $40,000–150,000
Top level: $500,000–$1,000,000

JOB DESCRIPTION: The jockey agent is the matchmaker of horse racing. He is the person who matches the jockeys with the horses.

As the name implies, the jockey agent works for the jockey. The agent talks with horse owners and trainers, selling the abilities of his client to get the most out of the horse during his next ride. The agent is compensated by receiving a percentage of the jockey's winnings.

The most successful agents represent a few different jockeys, or have one or two who win a lot of money consistently. The best relationships are true partnerships, with the agent evaluating the horses and working to get his jockeys better horses to ride and the jockey doing his best to give each and every horse he rides a chance to win the race. Together, a top jockey and top agent can earn millions of dollars.

KEYS TO GETTING THE JOB:
• Intimate knowledge of horse racing.
• Experience in judging horses and evaluating races.
• Familiarity with the network of owners and trainers.

POSITION: Announcer

EDUCATION/TRAINING: Experience in radio or television as broadcaster.

SALARY: Intro: $80 per day
Average: $150 per day
Top level: $400 per day

JOB DESCRIPTION: Track announcers are the fan's link to the action on the track. They are a combination of play-by-play broadcaster and public-address announcer. On the one hand, they must be able to provide an accurate, exciting call of each race to let the fans know how their horse is progressing. On the other, they must be able to manage the flow of information from the track to the stands about such things as special track activities, upcoming races, horses, trainers, jockeys and owners, race results, minutes to post time, and payouts. It is a critical position at any racetrack, very high-profile, and is therefore one of the highest-paid positions at the facility.

Announcers typically work seasonally and are paid by the day.

Most of the better ones work at more than one facility in a year. In addition, many track announcers host television replay shows, act as emcee for track functions, and serve as goodwill ambassadors for the track, all of which can increase their compensation. To most race fans, the track announcer is the sound of racing at that track.

KEYS TO GETTING THE JOB:
• Experience in broadcasting, on either radio or television.
• Racing experience, which may be obtained at smaller tracks or fair meetings on a part-time or fill-in basis. Eventually, you will be able to move up to a larger facility.

POSITION: Clerk of scales

EDUCATION/TRAINING: No specific background required.

SALARY: Intro: $50 per day
Average: $100 per day
Top level: $150 per day

JOB DESCRIPTION: The basic idea behind handicapping horses for racing is to make the better horses in a race carry some additional weight. This slows them down a little so that the race will be more even. The clerk of scales is the race official who weighs the jockeys before and after races to make sure the proper weight is being carried. If the jockey weighs less than the weight assigned, the balance is made up with lead pads inserted in a pouch beneath the saddle.

KEYS TO GETTING THE JOB:
• Familiarity with horsemen and horse racing.
• Ability to exist with trainers and jockeys.

POSITION: Clocker

EDUCATION/TRAINING: No specific background required.

SALARY: Intro: $50 per day
Average: $100 per day
Top level: $150 per day

JOB DESCRIPTION: The clockers at a racetrack time the morning workouts of the horses, then relay this information to the trainers and the media. Workout times are very important to trainers in order to gauge the progress of the athletes, while the media needs the information so they will be able to provide it to handicappers. Workouts take place from daybreak to about 10:00 A.M., seven days a week.

Since clockers are typically finished with their responsibilities early in the day, they often hold down another job at the track as well, such as clerk of scales. By combining these jobs and traveling from one track to another following the different meets, clockers can work steadily throughout the year and make a decent living.

KEYS TO GETTING THE JOB:
• Ability to identify each and every horse at the racetrack.
• Good relationships with trainers and media.

POSITION: Controller

EDUCATION/TRAINING: Degree in finance, accounting, or business.

SALARY: Intro: $30,000
Average: $50,000
Top level: $80,000

JOB DESCRIPTION: The controller or chief financial officer at a racetrack is the person responsible for managing the financial side of the racing business. Because of the large amount of money involved in wagering and the fact that the industry is regulated by the state, this is one of the key positions in racing.

The first level of responsibility for the controller is the day-to-day running of the business. This means insuring that payrolls are met on time, taxes are paid, and accounts receivable and accounts payable are well managed.

The second level of responsibility is managing the relationship between the handle, or the amount wagered on any given day, and the purses, or the amount paid out in prizes for each race. The daily handle is what drives the business. The state gets a percentage of the handle for its share, and the horsemen get a percentage for racing purses. The controller's goal at the end of the racing season is to break even. If the handle is up, purses are increased. If the handle is down, purses may be cut. The bigger the purses get, the better the athletes competing for those purses get. And as the quality of the racing improves, so does the attendance, which increases the handle even more. On the other hand, if the handle is down, the controller may decide to supplement the purses with other budgets to keep the quality of racing stable.

Unlike many other jobs in racing, the hiring of qualified financial managers from other industries, especially other entertainment entities, is not uncommon. Also, candidates from good educational programs do get the chance to enter the financial area perhaps a bit more readily than in other departments at a racetrack, due to the amount of work available in this area.

KEYS TO GETTING THE JOB:
• Strong educational, financial background.
• Experience in racing, facilities, or entertainment financial management a plus.

POSITION: General manager

EDUCATION/TRAINING: Degree in business or management preferred.

SALARY: Intro: $50,000
Average: $70,000
Top level: $250,000

JOB DESCRIPTION: The general manager or chief executive officer at a racing facility is in charge of all of the activities that take place there. The job includes developing and managing the budget; overseeing hundreds and sometimes thousands of full- and part-time staff people; working with the state regulatory agencies, horsemen, breeders, and media; and making sure that the track is a safe, convenient, fun, and exciting place to go for the fans—and, of course, that it is profitable for the company.

With very few exceptions, a facility general manager is a full-time employee of the track. In addition to the responsibilities he has during the racing season, the GM is also often involved in long-term planning and capital-improvement projects. If the legislature has some questions about racing in the state, it is the GM who is called to the capital to answer them. Along with the horsemen, the general manager is the spokesperson for racing in that community.

Becoming a general manager requires a solid foundation in the business of racing. This can be obtained by working at racetracks at lower levels and working your way up. Or, you can start by managing smaller meetings, such as the summer fair circuit. Or you can enroll in a racing management program, such as the one at the University of Arizona. Many of the GMs in racing today are graduates of that program.

KEYS TO GETTING THE JOB:
• Experience in managing budgets.
• Experience in managing people, including large numbers of part-time employees.

• Exposure to racing, either through work at a racetrack, a state regulating body, or an educational program.

POSITION: Mutuels director

EDUCATION/TRAINING: No specific requirements, but a good knowledge of computers and systems would be very helpful.

SALARY: Intro: $75 per day
Average: $125 per day
Top level: $200 per day

JOB DESCRIPTION: The mutuels director is the person responsible for overseeing the collection of the wagers and the distribution of the winnings to the fans. All of the people at the windows taking bets are under the control of the mutuels director. These can number anywhere from a few dozen at the smallest facility to over a thousand at a large track for a major event.

Wagering is the real business of racing, and the mutuels director is in charge of making sure it runs smoothly. Given the millions and millions of dollars in cash that change hands every week at a racing facility, keeping track of each transaction is a big challenge. The introduction of computer wagering systems has made the job of monitoring the transactions easier. The biggest part of the job today is managing the people behind the windows. The mutuels director can have a great impact on the profitability of the track just by being an expert scheduler. He must make sure there are just enough clerks working to handle the volume of business for that day. If he underestimates, there may be long lines of bettors and people unable to place their bets. If he overestimates, clerks will be getting paid for sitting idle most of the day.

A career as mutuels director usually starts by one's being a mutuels clerk. As with many jobs in racing, it is often easier to get a higher-level job at a smaller track, then make a lateral move to a bigger facility. A good educational background will help.

KEYS TO GETTING THE JOB:
• Educational background in computers especially helpful.
• Experience in working with computers.
• Good people-management skills.

POSITION: Racing secretary

EDUCATION/TRAINING: No specific educational requirements, but an extensive knowledge of horses and racing is a must.

SALARY: Intro: $35,000
Average: $50,000
Top level: $85,000

JOB DESCRIPTION: The racing secretary is one of the most important people in racing. It is the racing secretary who balances the needs of the horsemen and the track to build a competitive and entertaining racing schedule every day. He oversees the entering of horses each morning, is responsible for the recruitment of horses, and writes the condition book, the calendar of races that the track will present.

The racing secretary is very close to the horsemen at the track. In many cases, he serves as the "landlord" for these tenants, working with them to assign stall space and even handling disputes when they come up. The key to success for any good racing secretary is knowing the condition of each of the horses in the area that is eligible to race. With that knowledge, he will be able to build a competitive schedule of races. And to get that kind of information, the owners and trainers of the horses have to trust him and believe in his desire to treat them fairly.

In short, a horse race is really the racing secretary's show. He seeks out the competitors and puts them together in a combination he thinks will result in close, competitive, exciting races.

Getting a job as a racing secretary usually requires moving up through the ranks of track officials. This ultimately leads to a job of racing steward, then maybe to assistant racing secretary, then to director of racing or racing secretary. There are really no shortcuts in this career pathway. The amount of knowledge and experience required to build a meeting-long series of good races takes time to obtain. For those willing to pay the price, however, it is one of the most exciting jobs in racing.

KEYS TO GETTING THE JOB:
• Thorough knowledge of horses and racing.
• Experience as a racing official.
• Ability to mediate between groups with differing opinions.

POSITION: Starter, assistant starter

EDUCATION/TRAINING: No particular requirements.

SALARY: Intro: $75 per day
                 Average: $150 per day
                 Top level: $275 per day

JOB DESCRIPTION: The starter, as the title implies, is the person who starts the races. Starting is one of the most dangerous jobs at the track, since thoroughbred race horses are prone to be skittish in the starting gate and have been known to raise up and even fall in the gate, injuring jockeys and assistant starters in the process.

It is the responsibility of the starter to make sure the horses are all loaded properly into their correct starting gate and that they get off cleanly. It is a delicate job, trying to judge that split second when each horse is ready to go. The starter wants each horse to have an equal chance to win, which means he must wait for all the horses to be poised and ready to race. Wait too long, however, and they will all begin fussing in the gate and the race will be ruined before it begins.

The starter manages a group of assistant starters, the people who are actually on the gate helping the jockey position the horse for the start. It is the assistant starter who holds the horse's head straight and gives the starter the sign that the horse is ready. He is there to protect the jockey in case a horse flips, and is therefore susceptible to injury himself.

The starter also supervises the training of horses in the starting procedure. Horses have to be trained to run from the starting gate. Once they have practiced and mastered this skill, the starter checks them out. If he is satisfied that they can start a race safely, he will give his approval for them to race. No horse can race without this approval. Once a horse has gotten the approval to start that first time, it doesn't need to get it again unless it has a problem at the gate. In that case, it may have to receive some more training and be approved by the starter again.

Virtually all starters began their careers as assistant starters. Assistant starters have an extensive knowledge and a great deal of experience in dealing with thoroughbred horses. It is also a somewhat physical position, requiring the strength to manage the horse during loading and in the starting gate. Getting that experience is usually an outgrowth of being around horses from an early age, working with the trainers, walking and grooming horses, and in general being a part of the horse racing family. Once you have demonstrated an ability to handle the horses, you may be given a chance to be an assistant starter.

KEYS TO GETTING THE JOB:
• Experience with race horses.
• Being strong enough to handle the horses in the gate.

POSITION: Steward

EDUCATION/TRAINING: College degree preferred.

SALARY: Intro: $100 per day
                   Average: $175 per day
                   Top level: $300 per day

JOB DESCRIPTION: The racing steward is the referee of horse racing. Positioned along the racetrack, the steward is on the lookout for rules infractions by horses or jockeys. Sometimes, the steward will rule that the actions of a rider affected the outcome of a race and will disqualify him.

Each race is supervised by three stewards, one of whom is an employee of the state. Each decision is made by all three stewards, with the majority ruling. It is through this system that horse racing protects the integrity of each race.

Becoming a steward requires a thorough understanding of the rules of racing. Many stewards get their start at smaller racetracks or by working at races held at county fairs. If they show they have a good eye and can tell the difference between the frequent bumping that is a part of racing and that which gives a horse an unfair advantage, they will get the opportunity to move up.

KEYS TO GETTING THE JOB:
• Educational background.
• Knowledge of the rules of racing.
• Some horse racing experience.

HOSPITALITY MANAGER

POSITION: Hospitality manager

EDUCATION/TRAINING: No formal training needed.

SALARY: Intro: $18,000
Average: $30,000
Top level: $60,000

JOB DESCRIPTION: Hospitality is very important to the business of sports. It refers to the entertainment of people at a sporting event. Events often set up hospitality areas—tents or fenced-in spaces where companies and organizations can serve food and beverages and do business in an informal setting.

For example, take a typical NASCAR race. The hospitality area contains a couple of rows of large tents, each the same size, with perhaps a nice fence around them. They are each sponsored by a different company and brightly decorated to identify them. There is a Budweiser tent, an STP tent, a Goodyear tent, a Winston tent, and as many as twenty or thirty others.

Each hospitality tent serves as the headquarters for that company's activities for the weekend. The firm may host a large group of suppliers or one hundred of its best customers, or it may simply have decided to reward its employees. One day the tent may be used for a large political delegation, the next for a group of underprivileged kids.

Inside, companies offer a wide variety of food and beverages to their guests. In one tent, they may have tables set up with white tablecloths and serve shrimp cocktails, Maine lobster, and champagne. In the next tent, they may barbecue hot dogs and have cold beer and salads. It all depends on the company, the kind of budget it wants to put behind the event, and what it hopes to get out of it.

The coordination of all this activity is the job of the racetrack hospitality manager. It is a job of hundreds of details, most of them relating to preparation and setup of the facility, food service, staffing, and cleanup. It is something like throwing fifty separate parties, or opening fifty little restaurants for one week only. All of them have the same basic requirements, but each also has individual, special needs that must be met.

Full-time hospitality managers are usually affiliated with a facility, a team, or a promoter. Some have set up their own hospitality businesses and work under contract at a variety of activities, including sporting events. Often their job includes selling companies on the benefits of not only using their hospitality services but of hiring them to manage the event.

Getting a job in hospitality requires a great deal of experience in setting up and working with food service and hospitality facilities. Fortunately, this kind of experience is readily available. Every hospitality manager is looking for people to work part-time, during a specific season, or in entry-level positions. The business requires a lot of part-time help, jobs that are prone to high turnover. Do some homework in your area and find out who does the best job with hospitality. They may or may not be affiliated with sports—maybe they specialize in working with film crews on location, or doing business conventions. It doesn't matter, since the task at hand is the same. Join that firm part-time, such as after work or on weekends, work hard, and look around. Learn how it does things, how it makes money, how it interviews and hires people, how it gets contracts. Again, because of the nature of the business, a hospitality manager who finds someone competent will soon give him all the responsibility he can handle. And once you have gotten some good experience in a few different areas of the business, you will be ready to get a full-time position in sports hospitality.

WHERE THE JOBS ARE: Metropolitan areas; large venues such as racetracks and stadiums; special-event locations, such as golf courses for major tournaments.

KEYS TO GETTING THE JOB:
• Knowledge of food service operations.
• Good head for details.
• Ability to manage large groups of volunteers and part-time staff members.

JOURNALISM

POSITION: Sportwriter/columnist

EDUCATION/TRAINING: College degree in journalism preferred.

SALARY: Intro: $10,000
                Average: $40,000
                Top level: $250,000

JOB DESCRIPTION: For many sports fans, the highlight of their day is the time they spend reading about their favorite sports in their local newspaper. The information they get from their local sportswriter is what they talk about during their coffee break or on their bus ride home. The sportswriter is their contact with the inner workings of the team, an insider who lets them know what is really going on. While TV is king in the area of news delivery, it is in the newspaper sports pages and through the words of the sportswriter that sports fans get the bulk of their information.

Just about every newspaper in the country includes sports as part of its daily offering. At small newspapers, the sports reporter will also cover other areas, such as the police beat. At the large, big-city dailies, sports departments can number over twenty people.

At the top of the sportswriting job ladder are the columnists, people who produce a set number of feature stories each week on subjects of their own choosing. This is followed by the job of beat writer. These are writers who are assigned to specific teams or sports in their area. They have one job, and that is to report anything and everything that happens to that team. They are expected to generate day-of-game stories and to write features about the team on their beat. They are also expected to stay on top of all the breaking news stories in that sport all year long.

Most of the other writing is done by a pool of staff writers, who are assigned to stories on a daily basis by the sports editor. In many cases, a staff writer will develop a specialty, and all stories relating to that specialty are then assigned to him or her. There aren't enough stories to constitute a beat, per se, but they are important enough to warrant some concentrated coverage for part of the year. Golf and tennis events often fall in that category. When the PGA golf tour stops in town, the same writer covers that story all week and does it every year. When the tour leaves, the writer goes back to covering general assignments.

The job of sportswriters is to tell a story, a story about sports that is interesting, informative, and entertaining. It sounds like a lot of fun, and it is. But, there are two catches.

The first is, they have to do it every day. Day in and day out. A columnist especially feels this. You write a column on Monday about a Special Olympics athlete. Great stuff, award-winning stuff. What about Tuesday? Well, on Tuesday, you do a story on the local football team. It's an okay story, nothing great. What are you going to come up with for Wednesday? After that, what are you going to do on Thursday, and Friday, and next Monday? And day after day after day. Most of the time, there are enough topics to stimulate your creativity. Sports changes enough day to day to supply enough grist for the mill. But every writer knows the frustration of staring at a computer screen or a typewriter for an hour, trying to come up with an idea. It can be a real problem. And the reason it can be a problem is because of the second catch—the deadline.

Newspapers are printed and delivered every day. Getting the paper to a reader's door by 6:30 every morning is dependent on everyone's adhering to a very strict time schedule. For example, let's say the presses have to roll by midnight. It is a physical fact—if they don't start at that time, they can't print enough papers. If the presses have to roll at midnight, that means the paper has to be laid out and typeset by 11:00 P.M. Again, that is how long it takes; it can't be changed. That means a writer's story has to be completed and sent to the editor by the deadline, which in our hypothetical case is 10:00 P.M. Not 10:01; 10:01 is too late. If you get it in at 10:01, it will not be accepted. There are no excuses. A deadline is a deadline.

Ask any ten writers what they most dislike about their job and eight will tell you the pressure of the deadline. All sportswriters are used to "writing under deadline," as it's called. Some handle it better than others. Many people find out early in their careers that they can't handle deadline pressure. But it is a constant source of pressure for a newspaper or wire service writer, and is something you should be prepared for.

Getting a job as a sportswriter requires a solid journalistic background. This can be obtained by attending one of the many fine journalism colleges around the country. Internships at newspapers or magazines, which give you a chance to gain some experience, are sometimes available through these programs. Also, many colleges have their own newspapers, offering writers a chance to cover the various sports teams at the school.

After graduation, aspiring sportswriters take one of two pathways. They either take small jobs at larger publications or more substantial jobs at smaller publications. The latter is the most often recommended course of action. By moving to a small town and working for the local newspaper, you will have a chance to cover a lot of different teams and events, and to get more of your work in print. At a large newspaper, it is easy to become lost, to spend years doing high school sports wrap-ups and not ever getting the chance to write anything substantial.

Once you have established a body of work in a smaller publication, it is relatively easy to begin applying for jobs with larger newspapers and magazines.

To reach the top of the profession is a slow, steady climb, often requiring a series of job moves and relocations. But it is a pathway that is proven, and for those with talent the journey can be relatively short.

Magazine writers and writers for other publications have the same background as newspaper writers. In fact, most sports magazine writers started out in the newspaper business. Magazine writers are much more feature-oriented, and don't have to work under the kind of deadline pressure most sports journalists face. The career pathways are very similar—starting out with smaller publications and working your way to bigger ones once you have established yourself. Many writers get their start with magazines by doing one or two free-lance articles for them. If the magazine likes their work, they will keep assigning them stories. Eventually, this leads to an offer of a permanent job.

KEYS TO GETTING THE JOB:

- Strong educational background, with a journalism major.
- Writing experience. Work on your college newspaper or as stringer for a wire service, free-lance for a local daily, or contribute to a local weekly.
- Willingness to move from job to job, in order to get better assignments at bigger papers.
- Thorough sports knowledge.
- Ability to write on a deadline.

POSITION: Editor

EDUCATION/TRAINING: College degree in journalism preferred.

SALARY: Intro: $10,000
Average: $40,000
Top level: $150,000

JOB DESCRIPTION: The job of the editor is twofold. His or her responsibility is to help writers identify what stories to write. The sports editor at a newspaper, for example, will assign writers to each sporting event that he considers newsworthy. Further, the editor will tell the writer what kind of story to write, whether it is a "story of the game" or a feature story. He may also give the reporter an idea of how long he wants the story to be, and may assign a photographer to accompany him to take pictures relevant to the story.

The second part of the editor's job comes into play once the story has been written. The editor makes sure the story is in the correct format, that its content is technically correct with no spelling or grammatical errors, and that it is of the proper length. The editor may also have the writer rework part of the story. It is the editor who has the final say on what goes in and what stays out of a publication.

Becoming an editor requires developing much the same kind of expertise as a writer has. They are ultimately after the same thing—a good story well told. Editing skills can be taught, and are offered as part of any journalism program. While many people serve as both writer and editor, especially in smaller publications, it is possible to focus your career entirely on editing.

The pathway is much the same as it is for a writer. For example, after graduation from journalism school you start out editing high school stories for a small community newspaper. You then move to editing regular sports stories. This is followed by a stint as sports editor of the daily newspaper in a small town. Eventually, you work your way up to a job as an editor with a major newspaper or publication.

WHERE THE JOBS ARE: Newspapers with sports sections; sports magazines.

KEYS TO GETTING THE JOB:
• Degree in journalism with emphasis on editing.
• Willingness to start at a smaller publication to get some experience.
• Readiness to change jobs a few times to keep moving up.

LEAGUE MANAGEMENT

POSITION: Professional league management

EDUCATION/TRAINING: College degree; master's preferred.

SALARY: Intro: $22,000
Average: $50,000
Top level: $1,000,000 plus

JOB DESCRIPTION: The major professional sports teams are grouped into various leagues: the National Football League, the National Hockey League, Major League Baseball, the National Basketball Association. Each of these leagues is made up of a group of team owners, who hold the franchises enabling them to operate in a city and compete against other teams. The league staff is empowered by the owners to help them administer their sport.

This, in simple terms, is what the employees of the league do—manage the teams in the league. With the growth of professional sports, the huge amount of television and other revenue involved, and the complex nature of pro sports today, the number of people working in professional sports at the league level is in the hundreds.

The types of jobs available with a league depend on its role in its sport. Many of the day to day operational needs of a sport are handled at the league level. This includes building the game schedule for the league, a task which is much more difficult than might first appear. Each team has its own idea of when it should be in town and when it should travel, where it should be on holidays, and so on. Putting this information together and coming up with a schedule everyone can live with is almost a year-round process. The league also oversees officiating, making sure that the officials get to where they are supposed to be, that they are properly trained, and that there is always a group of new officials ready to come into the sport.

The league also works closely with the players. This includes things such as answering eligibility questions, mediating salary disputes, and most importantly of all, working with the labor unions and the various collective-bargaining agreements.

The league is also responsible for putting on events such as playoffs, championships, and all-star games. The league works with the host team to make sure all of the details get taken care of well before the event, and then about two weeks prior to its taking place league officials come in and manage the final details.

Today's leagues are also heavily involved in merchandising, marketing, and sponsorships. They have set up a separate parts of their organizations to handle these areas, groups such as NFL Properties and NBA Properties. The job of these groups is to raise awareness of the sport and generate revenue for the league and member clubs.

Managing information about the league and its teams through a public relations staff; creating publications, programs and other printed materials; and working with the media covering events and championships are also handled by league staffers.

Finally, enforcing the rules of the sport, making sure the owners and the players adhere to the guidelines they have agreed to compete under, falls under the jurisdiction of the league.

The major leagues are led by one person, acting as commissioner or executive director. Under that person are some senior executives, and under them are directors and department heads who run the business day to day. Like many franchise operations, the owners make a lot of decisions themselves by committee, and then leave the execution of their policy to the commissioner and his staff.

Jobs at the league level are usually filled by people who have spent time working at the franchise level. However, all the leagues have some entry-level positions, and many have had extensive internship programs for some time. Many people working in baseball around the country started in the Major League Baseball executive training program, for example.

Typically, league jobs require the employee to have a great deal of contact with many or all of the teams in the league. Often, they require a lot of traveling around the country to visit teams. And virtually the entire staff works and attends championship events such as the Super Bowl and the Stanley Cup finals.

WHERE THESE JOBS ARE: New York City.

KEYS TO GETTING THE JOB:
• Experience with a major league team.
• An internship with the league.
• Specific expertise in a defined discipline that teams typically don't have, such as law or journalism.

LUXURY BOX SALES/MANAGEMENT

POSITION: Luxury box sales/management

EDUCATION/TRAINING: Sales experience.

SALARY: Intro: $18,000
Average: $30,000
Top level: $60,000

JOB DESCRIPTION: It is widely believed that a big part of the reason Al Davis moved the Raiders to L.A. was in order to take advantage of the revenue that could be generated through the sale of luxury suites. While this didn't work out as well as Mr. Davis planned, it points to something that is now a fact of life in sports: luxury suites and boxes are a great source of revenue for team owners and promoters.

In stadiums and arenas all across the country, suites are being put into plans for building or remodeling existing facilities. Once they are completed, they can generate millions of dollars for an owner at no additional cost, and it is money the owner doesn't have to share with anyone.

The sale of luxury suites is a cross between the sale of a ticket package and that of an apartment. The ticket salesman talks about the excitement of having the best seat in the house for every game or event in the building, and being an important supporter of the team. The apartment salesman talks about the various amenities of the suite, the pampering service, how comfortable, warm, cool, and convenient it is. Together, they make a compelling case for buying or leasing a luxury suite.

Because of the revenue potential of luxury suites, teams and facilities are now assigning people to handle the sale and management of them full-time. It is a job that enables you to meet and work with a lot of high-level businesspeople (and that will quickly acquaint you with how demanding they can be). At facilities that have had suites in place for a long time, you end up being in the renewal business, making sure your customers are happy enough to sign up for another lease period. At new facilities, it is the long process of convincing people that the suite is worth the premium price, and coming up with creative ways they can use the suite to make it even more cost-effective.

Since it is a relatively new field, people with experience selling sports suites are hard to find. Therefore, for you to get started, it is usually advantageous to have some experience in sales and some familiarity with the hospitality business. With that, and a familiarity with how and why corporations entertain, you will be a good candidate for this job.

WHERE THE JOBS ARE: Teams and facilities across the country, including some college facilities.

KEYS TO GETTING THE JOB:
• Sales experience.
• Knowledge of how corporate entertaining can help a company.
• Ability to listen to prospective clients' problems and goals and apply them to use of a luxury suite.

MAILROOM MANAGER

POSITION: Mailroom manager

EDUCATION/TRAINING: No specific training required.

SALARY: Intro: $15,000
Average: $24,000
Top level: $30,000

JOB DESCRIPTION: In the show *How to Succeed in Business Without Really Trying*, our hero J. Pierrepont Finch starts his climb up the corporate ladder in the mailroom. He eventually ends his journey in the executive suite, complete with a key to the executive washroom.

The mailroom exists as an entry-level position in sports, too. The volume of mail sent and received every day by a major league team, league, or other sports organization is enormous. It requires a specific person to handle the load.

The job of the mailroom manager is fairly cut-and-dried. Pick things up at the post office, sort them, deliver them. Gather all the outgoing mail and packages, apply the correct postage, send it out. The two key things to remember are that you are getting to know everyone in the organization and that you are already a member of the company. When jobs in other departments open up, candidates from within the company are considered first, so you already have a leg up on everyone else.

The job of mailroom coordinator is in and of itself not exactly a challenging sports career. But as a stepping-stone, as our friend Finch found out, it can lead to something really outstanding.

WHERE THE JOBS ARE: Any large sports organization, most of which are in metropolitan areas.

KEYS TO GETTING THE JOB:
• Persistence in applying. Turnover in this spot is fairly high.
• Upbeat personality.
• Good organizational skills.

MANAGEMENT

POSITION: Sports manager/front office

EDUCATION/TRAINING: Degree in sports management, business.

SALARY: Intro: $15,000
              Average: $40,000
              Top level: $500,000

JOB DESCRIPTION: Sports managers, like managers in any other form of business, usually don't start out as managers at all. They start in a specific department of a company or doing a particular task. They then get promoted, or change jobs, and wind up supervising someone. As their career progresses, more and more people fall under their control, until eventually they become full-time managers, overseeing the staff members who carry out their directions.

A job as a sports manager is the same as the job of manager in any other profession—to manage resources. Most often, these resources include two main components: people and money.

The sports manager is responsible for finding, hiring, training, managing, and providing growth opportunities for his or her employees. On the money side, he or she is charged with setting and managing the budget, which allocates the financial resources available to achieve the goals of the organization.

The job of manager is included here not because it is a place to start a sports career, but because it is a good sports position to aspire to.

As an example of a modern-day sports managerial career pathway, we'll look at the career of Andy Dolich, the vice president of business operations for the Oakland A's.

Andy went to college at American University in Washington, D.C., where he played some basketball and soccer. While there, he

worked in the school athletic department, and began thinking there
might be a way to make sports a career. He read about a graduate
degree program in sports administration at Ohio University. He
applied and was accepted.

While at Ohio U., he did an internship with the Philadelphia
76ers in season-ticket sales. It was the perfect match. The 76ers got
someone at a very low cost who would work like crazy to get
experience and succeed. He so impressed them that after graduation
he was hired full-time in season-ticket sales.

Keep in mind, this was 1972, and the 76ers were the worst team
in the NBA. In his first year there, the team was 9–73. The first
month of the season it didn't win a game. Nor did it win a game in
the last month of the season. But he worked hard, putting in many
long hours, and was eventually promoted to the position of assistant
to the general manager. Salary: $7,000 per year.

He spent one year with the 76ers, learning as much as he could and
being as active in the community as possible. His efforts were noticed
by a prominent Philadelphia businessman who ran an NASL soccer
team in Tampa Bay and was starting an indoor box lacrosse team in
Washington, D.C., known as the Washington Arrows. He wanted
Andy to work for him and gave him his choice of situation. He chose
lacrosse, for several instructive reasons: it was new, it was a start-up
company, and it was more of a challenge. Andy knew that he would
have more of an opportunity to advance quickly and gain more
responsibility, in a young, struggling organization. He started as
business manager and soon became the administrative vice president.

After three years in lacrosse, the league was folding. Again,
he had worked on developing contacts and a reputation within the
community, and was hired by the Washington Capitals hockey team
as its director of marketing. He stayed there three years, until he
had a disagreement with the owner about how the team should be
marketed. He left the club, only to be hired as the vice president of
marketing for the Washington Diplomats soccer team. Soon, he was
named executive vice president and general manager.

Near the end of 1980, Madison Square Garden Corporation, which
owned the Dips, decided to get out of the soccer business. At about
the same time, the Haas family of San Francisco bought the Oakland

A's from Charlie Finley. They are the owners of Levi's jeans, and were looking for someone to head up their baseball business operation. Through a headhunter, they found Dolich, who was hired as the vice president of business, the position he holds today. He now manages a staff of forty full-time people and a budget in the millions of dollars, and he has a World Series Championship ring to boot.

Overall, Andy Dolich's career has covered over twenty years. He has had five jobs in three parts of the country. He has been on the brink of disaster several times, with teams and leagues folding from under him. He has been with clubs that set records for futility and clubs that have won championships. And he has made a comfortable living for himself and his family. Altogether, it has been a very typical experience in the volatile world of sports management.

The career of Andy Dolich is a good example of the career pathway of sports managers in the nineties. With the proliferation of college sports administration programs, sports organizations have the luxury of being able to hire highly qualified young people to fill entry-level management positions. They gain some experience, then either move up the organization or join another group at a higher level. Since sports organizations are not very large and tend to have little turnover, it is not at all unusual for people to change jobs several times in order to advance in their career.

As the business of sports becomes more and more businesslike, the need for qualified managers is increasing. By building a solid foundation of education and experience, the sports administrator of tomorrow will be able to take advantage of opportunities as they present themselves.

WHERE THE JOBS ARE: Sports organizations, teams, facilities, corporations, media companies, any business involved in sports.

KEYS TO GETTING THE JOB:
• Educational background in sports administration, business management; master's degree preferred.
• Willingness to start at the bottom to learn the business and gain experience, and to move from job to job around the country as opportunities present themselves.

MANUFACTURER'S REPRESENTATIVE

POSITION: Manufacturer's representative

EDUCATION/TRAINING: Sales training preferred.

SALARY: Intro: $15,000
Average: $40,000
Top level: $150,000 plus

JOB DESCRIPTION: The job of manufacturer's representative in this case refers to a person who sells sporting goods and equipment.

The kinds of equipment and supplies used in sports are many and varied. Almost without exception, though, if a manufacturer makes it he will require someone to sell it to his customers. This is as true for AstroTurf and race car engines as it is for golf balls and tennis rackets.

A typical sales rep will have a product or line of products, and will sell those products within a certain territory. For example, a representative for a tennis manufacturer will sell its rackets, clothing, and other products in a territory that may be as small as the city of Portland or as large as the East Coast. The representative calls on tennis clubs, sporting goods stores, and general merchandise stores to show them the product and get them to order some. He may offer special discounts, or offer to have a tennis racquet stringing demonstration set up in the store. Or he may agree to host and sponsor an exhibition tournament, featuring Ivan Lendl or Andre Agassi or one of the other professional players who endorse the product. All in the name of getting the merchandise out there.

Just as the kinds of sporting goods varies, so does the size and quality of sporting goods manufacturers. In general, though, the big, long-respected names in any particular industry got that way by having good products and treating their customers and employees well enough to keep everyone happy. You are probably safe in working for one of them.

The job of manufacturer's representative often includes a great deal of travel. You normally work out of your home, which puts you in the heart of your sales territory and able to see your customers easily. The position includes a large amount of client contact every day, making sales, providing information, and solving problems. Many times, reps get the chance to work closely with the professional teams and athletes who use their products. And with the right company and the right product, the job can be very lucrative. Sporting goods are a multibillion-dollar industry in this country. And on each billion, some sales rep somewhere is getting a commission. The potential for large earnings, the opportunity to work closely with teams and athletes, and the lack of specific educational qualifications or training make this career field attractive. If you can sell, you can sell sporting goods. And if you sell a lot of them, you will make a lot of money.

The important thing to remember when looking for a job of this kind is to be as selective as you can about the products you sell. If you represent a line no one has ever heard of, you will have little success selling it. Plus, it will add nothing to your resume; people are not impressed with how well you did selling Bill and Bob's sports shoes. However, if you join a large, well-known firm, chances are it will have some sort of training program for you, your products will have appeal no matter how good or bad a sales job you do initially, and if you do decide to change companies later on you will have gained wonderful experience. Jobs with great companies are, naturally, a bit tougher to get, but if you are willing to relocate and aren't too narrow in your choice of companies or products, you should be able to get a job relatively quickly.

WHERE THE JOBS ARE: Sporting goods manufacturers nationwide.

KEYS TO GETTING THE JOB:

- Some technical knowledge about sports and the supplies you intend to sell.
- Willingness to travel or relocate.
- Good communication skills.
- Professional appearance.

MARKET RESEARCH

POSITION: Market researcher

EDUCATION/TRAINING: Degree in statistics, math, business.

SALARY: Intro: $15,000
Average: $35,000
Top level: $80,000

JOB DESCRIPTION: Market research is becoming a more important part of the business of sports each year. As the dollars invested in sports increase, companies are looking for ways to predict results and thereby decrease risk. The best way to do this is through research.

Research is a discipline that is used in a lot of different sports industries. For example, advertising agencies use research to test the effectiveness of proposed ads for athletic shoes. Baseball teams use research to determine the demographic composition of their fan base. Media outlets like radio and television stations use research extensively, to come up with the audience numbers they use to set their advertising rates for college basketball. And corporations use research to determine which female tennis player they should choose to sell more of their products.

The market researcher can work for any of these groups, or can be a part of an independent research firm hired to gather information and provide analysis.

The researcher uses a variety of techniques to gather information. These include surveys, direct-mail diaries, focus groups, and questionnaires. The researcher helps the client identify exactly what problems or questions it wants to have answered, picks the appropriate research tool, and designs all of the questions. After the raw data is gathered, the researcher helps the client interpret the results.

By taking some of the guesswork out of the decision-making process, owners, general managers, and other sports executives can make better, more informed choices.

Getting a job in market research first requires a strong educational background. To work with the data, you need to have a good understanding of statistical principles. Once you have that, the best places to start are with large companies that do a lot of research, or with a pure research company. Entry-level positions would include managing the information-gathering process, working with focus groups, and writing research survey questions. After you obtain some solid business experience, you can begin to look for a position that offers you some exposure to the sport you like. This job may be with a company that sponsors that sport, a team that gathers a lot of information on its fan base, or a research company that specializes in sports-related research.

WHERE THE JOBS ARE: Advertising agencies, radio and television stations and networks, professional sports leagues, sports marketing firms, and professional research companies like Nielsen and Arbitron, which are both located in New York City.

KEYS TO GETTING THE JOB:
• Background or training in statistics.
• Familiarity with techniques of market research.
• Ability to interpret the results of research.

MARKETING

POSITION: Sports marketing director

EDUCATION/TRAINING: Degree in sports marketing, sports administration, or marketing. Master's degree preferred.

SALARY: Intro: $18,000
Average: $35,000
Top level: $250,000

JOB DESCRIPTION: Sports marketing means different things in different organizations. In general, it refers to the use of sports as a marketing tactic to influence consumers to do something. Examples are using NASCAR racing to encourage retailers to put up large displays of Tide laundry detergent, or using the broadcast of the Super Bowl to introduce the latest breakthrough in personal computers, or developing a direct-mail campaign to encourage fans to buy Tampa Bay Buccaneer season tickets.

The job of the sports marketer is usually, in the end, to sell something to someone. In sports, this can take many forms. The spectator sports have tickets to sell. The media has advertising to sell. Sponsoring companies have products to sell. Athletes and announcers have their talent to sell. Everyone is selling something. And who are they selling to? The fans.

Sports is a very effective vehicle for selling. The reasons are many, but the important ones are that fans form an emotional attachment to sports, they are loyal, and they "consume" sports in significant numbers.

The emotional attachment fans feel toward sports has been well documented over the years. Every time Brazil is eliminated from World Cup competition, some poor souls are so despondent they commit suicide. Athletes routinely get proposals of marriage from fans. Wearing the wrong shirt or even singing the wrong song can get you a black eye or worse at a football game between particularly strong rivals. Marketers try to take that emotional involvement and transfer it to whatever it is they are trying to sell. It can be anything. For example, a children's hospital in Houston may need money to purchase a kidney machine. It is one thing for the hospital administrator to get on television and ask for donations to this very worthy cause. But would this work better?

"Hi. I'm Warren Moon of the Houston Oilers. I'm asking for your support for a new kidney machine for the Houston Children's Center. To get things started, I'm going to make the first donation of one thousand dollars. And by the way, for every one of you who makes a donation, I will send you a football autographed by me and all of my teammates. Won't you please help?"

Sorry, doctor, no contest.

Fan loyalty comes into play here as well, because fan loyalty translates into brand loyalty. Advertisers pay huge amounts of money to get their signs in stadiums and arenas, not only to get their product served in the building, but to build their association with the teams that play there. If you see your favorite player drink a Coke in a commercial, see the huge Coke sign up in the building, and have collected a set of twelve Coca-Cola player mugs at your local fast-food restaurant chain, then Coke is the cola you are going to choose when you go to the grocery store. Many people, especially in the Southeastern part of the country, drive the same kind of car as their favorite NASCAR driver. They drive a Ford, they have always driven a Ford, and they won't change for any reason. Companies love that kind of brand loyalty.

The sheer number and variety of sports fans out there is also a key reason why sports marketing is such a big business. When over a hundred million people tune in to watch the Super Bowl, or the World Cup has an audience of over a billion people, your message is reaching a substantial part of the available audience for your product or service.

The job of sports marketing includes identifying the audience you want to reach, making strategic plans about how to reach them, choosing the best ways to carry out those plans, and then evaluating the results. More and more, companies, agencies, and even state and local governments are using sports marketing to accomplish their objectives in the marketplace.

To get a job in sports marketing requires a firm foundation in the principles of marketing. This can be obtained through a sports marketing or business school. Or it can be learned through experience, working with someone else who has a good knowledge of marketing. There is a large body of knowledge out there that is available to tap into, and enough standard principles and methods in the field to keep you from having to "reinvent the wheel" once you get into the business.

Jobs in sports marketing carry with them much of the responsibility for the success of failure of a sports entity. Since they are so important, they usually pay better and include more benefits than other sports jobs. Also, companies, teams, and organizations tend to have more people involved in sports marketing than in other departments, resulting in more of a hierarchy and a clearer career pathway to the top of the organization.

WHERE THE JOBS ARE: Teams, leagues, sports organizations, corporations, facilities, media outlets, colleges, event promoters.

KEYS TO GETTING THE JOB:
• Degree in sports marketing or business; MBA preferred, especially for entry-level jobs in corporations.
• Some experience in sports or event marketing, obtained either as a volunteer, in a part-time position, or as an intern.

MERCHANDISING MANAGEMENT

POSITION: Merchandising manager

EDUCATION/TRAINING: Degree in business, marketing.

SALARY: Intro: $20,000
Average: $40,000
Top level: $100,000

JOB DESCRIPTION: Sports merchandise is a billion-dollar industry in the U.S. today. Through outlets such as retail stores, mail-order catalogs, and concession stands, millions upon millions of T-shirts, caps, balls, pennants, stickers, and dozens of other items are sold every year. The people who work in this part of the sports business are known as merchandising managers.

Let's follow the life of a piece of sports merchandise, say an NBA T-shirt. First, the manufacturer has to obtain a license from the NBA, allowing him to produce the shirt with an NBA team logo on it. Once the shirt is produced, it is sold to an NBA team. The team then marks up the price and sells it to a fan. The people who handle all of these transactions are merchandising managers.

Merchandising managers work with things such as licensing agreements, the procurement of merchandise, and negotiating with suppliers and vendors, and many even handle the final distribution of the item. Most merchandise is sold as souvenirs, but some may be given away as premium items to attract fans to events.

The kinds of sports organizations that have merchandising managers are varied. The list includes most professional teams, most major sports facilities, college athletic departments, leagues, professional and amateur sports organizations, Halls of Fame, and racetracks. The list also includes all of the manufacturers and distributors of the sports merchandise. Think of all the places you can go to get a sports souvenir. A merchandising manager—and maybe two or three at different steps along the way—was responsible for getting it there.

The job of merchandising manager is very much one of inventory control. Long production lead times mean that planning is essential. The best merchandisers are able to anticipate what the next "hot" item will be, and on the flip side of the coin are able to identify when something is about to lose popularity. No one wants to get stuck with a warehouseful of Hula Hoops. On the other hand, no one wants to discover his main competitor has sold two million of the neon squeeze bottles you turned down six months ago because you thought no one would buy them.

Getting a job as a sports merchandising manager requires some experience in the field, usually gained by working for a manufacturer or merchandise distributor. These companies are always on the look-out for someone to sell their products or to help them manage inventory. Once you have some skills in pricing and negotiation, and have become familiar with the ebb and flow of the business, you will be ready to move into a sports merchandising job.

WHERE THE JOBS ARE: Teams, facilities, manufacturers, sports organizations of all kinds that have merchandise to sell.

KEYS TO GETTING THE JOB:
• Educational background.
• Some experience in merchandise manufacturing, retailing, or distribution.

OFFICIAL/REFEREE

POSITION: Professional official/referee/umpire

EDUCATION/TRAINING: College degree; graduate of training
school.

SALARY: Intro: $35,000
Average: $50,000
Top level: $100,000

JOB DESCRIPTION: Most officials, referees, umpires, and judges
work at the job only part-time. Even the highest-level college basketball referee or football official is only doing it as a sideline.

There are, however, some people in the professional sports who
do make their living by officiating. These are the baseball umpires,
basketball referees, hockey officials, and, to a lesser extent, football
referees. In addition, selected individuals in such sports as gymnastics, soccer, and tennis make a living as full-time officiators.

For anyone familiar with sports, the official is a familiar sight.
Throwing a flag for roughing the kicker. Signaling a one-shot foul,
before the shot. Calling strike three, on the outside corner of the
plate. Our awareness and love of the sports we follow is filled with
these and other phrases that officials use to define the limits of the
sport. It is their job to enforce the rules of the game—often to the
displeasure of loyal fans everywhere.

The job of professional sports officials includes a great deal of
travel. They work individually or in teams, and go from game to
game, event to event, making sure everyone is competing within the
rules. It can be a lonely profession. The fans, players, and other
people around the sport tend to keep an arm's length away from the
official. No one wants to get too close, both to avoid any appearances
of trying to influence the outcome of a competition and because it is

179

the nature of sports in this country that when things go wrong, the official is an easy target for blame. But the people involved in officiating truly love the sport, and love what they are doing.

Becoming a professional official, in any sport, requires starting at a lower level and working your way up. In sports like baseball, special schooling and training systems are in place to begin the process. Three schools for umpires are sanctioned by Major League Baseball. They are the Jim Evans Academy of Professional Umpiring in Chandler, Arizona; the Brinkman-Froemming Umpire School in Cocoa, Florida; and the Wendelstedt Umpire School in Ormond Beach, Florida. Other leagues, including the NBA and NFL, draw from other sources, like colleges and the CBA.

But once the training is over, it can mean year after year in the minor leagues, learning the ropes firsthand. In other sports, it can be game after game of junior high, high school, and college competition, both men's and women's, before you get the chance to hit the big time.

Getting started in officiating is really not difficult. Choose the sport you wish to get involved with. Learn the rules, and take advantage of any training programs or classes that may be available. Then get yourself a whistle and get started. You will find out soon enough if you have what it takes to keep striving for a professional career.

WHERE THE JOBS ARE: Major sports leagues, associations.

KEYS TO GETTING THE JOB:
• Proper training, education.
• Experience at lower levels.

PERSONNEL/HUMAN RELATIONS

POSITION: Personnel/human relations director

EDUCATION/TRAINING: Human resources degree; master's preferred.

SALARY: Intro: $15,000
Average: $40,000
Top level: $90,000

JOB DESCRIPTION: As the relatively young business of sports becomes larger, more expensive, and more professionalized, organizations from hockey leagues to domed stadiums are turning to human resource experts for guidance in the areas of hiring and managing their employees. This person is different from the one in charge of athlete recruitment. This person deals with what is commonly called the "front office," the people behind the scenes in sports.

The job of the human resource manager includes more than soliciting and reviewing resumes and insuring that people are hired and fired fairly. It also includes developing retirement and medical programs, managing profit-sharing plans, overseeing training, and in general helping to raise the level of professionalism in the industry.

To date, only the largest and most forward-thinking sports organizations have developed jobs in this area. But the list is growing, and someday all sports teams, leagues, events, and organizations will have a person or people filling this role.

The best way to get a job in sports human resource management is to start your career outside the industry. Go to work for a government agency in personnel, or a large entertainment or consumer-oriented company like an airline, or a public utility. These are the kinds of companies that are advanced in the area of human resource management. Once you have gained some experience, you will be able to make a lateral move into the sports field. Again, because sports is a young industry, and because it is a field that typically has many applicants for a few jobs, it has not dealt very well with personnel issues. Therefore, when a sports organization needs to find someone in this area, it tends to look for someone outside of sports. And that is where it will find you.

WHERE THE JOBS ARE: Major sports organizations, teams, events, facilities, corporations.

KEYS TO GETTING THE JOB:
• Expertise in human resource management.
• Familiarity with federal, state, and local laws and statutes governing employment.
• Ability to handle all aspects of human resources—being a generalist instead of a specialist.

PHOTOGRAPHER

POSITION: Photographer

EDUCATION/TRAINING: Training in sports photography.

SALARY: Intro: $12,000
Average: $30,000
Top level: $150,000

JOB DESCRIPTION: Nothing is quite as thrilling to a fan as an excellent sports photograph. For years, the pictures we have seen of miracle catches or outstanding finishes have moved and excited us.

Jobs as sports photographers take a couple of forms. The main one is the photojournalist, a person working for a newspaper, magazine, or wire service who takes sports pictures for his employer. This is the person you see at the games, the races, and other events, chronicling the action for the next edition.

The other form of work for photographers is as an independent contractor. He or she contracts with a team, a college, a corporation, or even an individual to shoot an event. This is how the top photographers in sports work. For example, Michael Zigaris in the Bay area has contracts with the teams to shoot the Oakland A's and the San Francisco 49ers. He takes all of the standard pictures of the players for the program, yearbook, brochures, and other publications. He attends every game, taking action photos that he then sells copies of to the team or to another buyer, if he can find one. For photographers like Michael, the majority of the income they receive is from people who want to use the photos he takes for advertisements or brochures, or for books and magazines.

Other photographers will contract to do feature projects. They may sign a contract with *Sports Illustrated* to photograph the annual swimsuit issue, for example. The entire job, with planning, processing, and editing, may take months to do and cost tens of thousands of dollars, all for one magazine issue.

Working as an independent contractor requires an established reputation as a sports photographer. Because of the fleeting nature of sports, the job of the photographer is a tough one. For example, George Long of Long Photography in Los Angeles once had an assignment to shoot the women's marathon Olympic trials. The shot they wanted, the only shot they would pay for, was of the winner crossing the finish line. He traveled over a thousand miles, set up five hours early, and waited in drizzling rain for the chance to get that one picture. Despite a crush of people at the finish line, he got the shot they needed.

Compensation for sports photographers starts fairly low. Even for established people with solid contacts, the compensation is relatively modest. The people at the very top of the profession, however, those who mix sports photography with studio work, can reach very high levels of income.

Starting a career as a sports photographer begins with training, education, and taking a lot of pictures. Most people in the business now got their start in college, shooting sports for the school newspaper or the athletic department. They then moved into photojournalism for a newspaper, wire service, or magazine. Some went into related fields, such as shooting winner's circle photos at a racetrack or taking pictures of athletes for collector card sets.

The important thing to remember is that it takes time, a lot of practice, and a lot of mistakes to become a successful sports photographer. In the beginning, you will probably not be making very much money. But if you love it, and if you have an eye for it, you will have the chance to take some of the most exciting pictures anyone will ever see, and quite possibly to make a lot of money.

WHERE THE JOBS ARE: Newspapers, wire services, sports magazines, professional and college teams, major events and tours.

KEYS TO GETTING THE JOB:
• Technical expertise. It is difficult enough to take a good shot—you can't afford to ruin it by misusing equipment or doing faulty processing.

• Experience. Practice makes perfect. Shoot whatever you can: high school football; Little League baseball; pictures for your college newspaper—anything and everything to build your portfolio. If you have talent, it will come through in your photographs, no matter what the subject.

PLAYER PERSONNEL

POSITION: Player personnel

EDUCATION/TRAINING: Playing or coaching experience.

SALARY: Intro: $12,000
Average: $30,000
Top level: $200,000

JOB DESCRIPTION: All professional sports franchises have an individual who handles the scouting, evaluation, and recruitment of new players for the team. He is the one who makes the number one draft pick, or signs the free-agent relief pitcher, or gets the much-needed point guard from the Continental Basketball Association. This individual is the player personnel director.

Teams acquire new players in three ways: through an organized draft, a trade with another team, or the signing of free agents. The talent pools include colleges and high schools, other teams in the league, or the minor leagues. It is the player personnel director's job to constantly be in touch with those talent pools, to evaluate talent, decide which players he wants on the team, and then sign them. In sports like baseball and hockey, after the athletes are under contract the player personnel department decides where they should be placed in the minor league system. They then work with coaches, instructors, and administrators to move players through the system, with the ultimate goal of having the player contribute to the major league team.

The day-to-day work in player personnel includes equal parts studying and networking. Through the study of film, videotape, scouting reports, and box scores, as a player personnel director you get a feel for the ability of players. But often that isn't the whole story. To fill in the gaps, you turn to an army of friends and contacts, including coaches, trainers, team doctors, high school friends of the athlete, full- or part-time scouts, other administrators—anyone who can give you reliable information about the player you are interested in. It is from these networking sources that you learn of a problem with drugs, or of an injury that won't go away, or of a desire to compete and win that is so strong it makes up for a lack of physical ability. These are often the factors that determine the level of contribution a player will make, and ultimately how the team will perform.

Understandably, these contacts and this trust take years to develop. But there are many opportunities to break into this area of sports. Much of the more time-consuming work can be done by someone with little experience. Breaking down film, conducting interviews with coaches and players, running tests, tracking performances of minor leaguers, and compiling scouting reports require expertise in the sport, but not necessarily a lot of experience. Of course, these jobs also don't pay very well. Many times, they don't pay anything at all. But as your experience grows and the weight of the decisions you make increases, so will your responsibility, and eventually your compensation (and the expectations of the owner and general manager).

Kirk Mee, director of pro player personnel for the Washington Redskins, started in football as a player at Wilmington College. He then received his master's degree from Ohio University and went into coaching. He started as an assistant and then moved to head coach at Defiance College in Ohio. After that, he served as an assistant for three years at the University of Wisconsin. Through contacts he made at Wisconsin, he was next hired by the Redskins to work in their scouting department, breaking down film of potential players. He added some duties in college scouting and eventually became a full-time scout. As his expertise grew and coaches changed at the team, he eventually was moved into his present position.

This is a typical example of a player personnel pathway. It begins with coaching experience on the high school, small-college, or major-college level, works into a part-time or low-level full-time scouting position, and, after a number of years, leads to a position as player personnel director.

A good way to break in is to volunteer to work part-time. Many teams use part-time help in the area of player personnel. For example, in football, part-time people are used to go through the hours and hours of game film on prospective college players. For a wide receiver, they may compile a video showing each time a ball was thrown in his area over the last two seasons. For an offensive lineman, they may put together all of his opportunities to pass-block. In this form, the player's ability is easier to evaluate. While these jobs are often tedious, they are a great way to learn about the evaluation of players and to get some experience.

WHERE THE JOBS ARE: Sports franchises or scouting services.

KEYS TO GETTING THE JOB:
• Experience as a player, coach, or scout in the sport.
• Proficiency in evaluating playing ability.
• Contacts in the sport are helpful, although not required.
• Patience to perform mundane tasks while learning the business.

PREMIUMS

POSITION: Premium/promotional item manager

EDUCATION/TRAINING: Retail sales, buying experience.

SALARY: Intro: $15,000
                Average: $30,000
                Top level: $60,000

JOB DESCRIPTION: Many teams, especially minor and major
league professional baseball teams, use promotional premium items
as giveaways to entice fans to games. Bat Night, Hat Night, Helmet
Night, GI Joe Action Figure Night—anything and everything that
has enough appeal to boost the gate is fair game. Managing the
selection, acquisition, and distribution of these items is the job of
the promotional item manager.

Selecting which premium items to distribute at an event or during
a season is an exercise in predicting the future. A few premium
nights are obvious and always work, such as Bat Night in baseball.
Every kid wants a baseball bat, they have a very high perceived
value, and they are fairly easy to obtain. The challenge comes when
you try to predict what will be hot six or eight months from now.
Because of the lead time needed for overseas production of the item,
that's how far into the future you need to project. If you do a poster
of your team for opening day, what do you do about the blockbuster,
three-player deal that has changed your whole lineup the week before? Maybe you'd like to do a tie-in with a children's television
show. A month before your 15,000 beach towels arrive, the show is
canceled. But on the flip side of things, you may find a new kind of
bright green hat that becomes the rage of the city, so much so that
you have to have a SECOND Green Hat Night just to keep your fans
happy.

Acquiring premium items makes up the bulk of the job. It requires constant contact with domestic and overseas suppliers, looking at samples to insure quality control, going through catalog after catalog of merchandise in search of the best items for your fans, negotiating the price of each item, setting production and delivery schedules and them monitoring them to make sure deadlines are met, sometimes even working with customs officials to ease the movement of your merchandise into the country. It requires a person who is very detail-oriented, is a good negotiator, and is a creative thinker.

Distribution of the items at the rink, racetrack, arena, or stadium is usually handled by a part-time or volunteer staff. This staff can be quite large, and requires some training in order to insure that items go to the right people: items for kids to kids, items sponsored by beer companies to adults, one item per customer, and so on. Nothing makes a fan angrier than showing up with a child for Bat Day and being told that the bats are all gone, then seeing an adult walk away from the game carrying seven of them.

Most promotional managers working in sports today got their jobs one of two ways. They either started with the premium item manufacturer or distributor and then moved to the team side, or they were one of those people at the gate handing out merchandise and moved up from there. A third pathway, coming from a sports admin-istration school, doing an internship with a team or facility, and then getting hired, is becoming more and more common.

WHERE THE JOBS ARE: Minor and major league baseball teams, NBA teams, CBA teams, NHL teams, racing facilities.

KEYS TO GETTING THE JOB:
• Experience with suppliers and manufacturers of merchandise.
• Good head for details.
• Background in working with kids; knowing what kids like.
• Good negotiation skills.

POSITION: Premium item supplier/manufacturer

EDUCATION/TRAINING: Degree in business; sales experience.

SALARY: Intro: $12,000
Average: $35,000
Top level: $150,000

JOB DESCRIPTION: The other side of the premium item equation is the supplier. Most premium items are manufactured overseas—in Taiwan or China, for example. These manufacturers have representatives in the United States selling their merchandise for them. The most active firms in the area of sports premium items take it a step farther: they take a bid order from a team and then find a manufacturer to fill it. A job with one of these supplier firms can be one of the most varied in sports.

Every major premium item supplier has on staff someone who specializes in working with sports teams. The key to success as a sports premium item supplier is the relationship you have with your customer, the team. It takes a great deal of confidence to place an order for 50,000 items, to be delivered on a specific date six months from now. The date will be advertised and people will come from miles away to get the item. If it isn't there, or if it is of poor quality, the team gets the blame. And the supplier loses the business forever. So a big part of the supplier's job is making sure the teams are happy and don't get any surprises. This requires a lot of communication with a lot of people. If your territory is a large one, it can mean having a close relationship with five or six people on every team in the country.

The rest of the job is DETAILS—making sure orders are taken correctly, instructions are clear, customs forms are filled out, delivery dates are firm, and problems are addressed before they become crises. Careful planning and preparation for the unexpected will lead to great success.

Compensation can be outstanding. Competition is tough, but because the number of items is so large the amount of money generated is considerable. With a generous sales incentive plan, an annual income in six figures is not unusual in this business.

To get started in the premium business, you should get an entry-level position in sales. Sales drives this business. No matter how good you are in other areas, like shipping, design, and manufacturing, you will never reach the top unless you are proficient at sales. Since most of the sales jobs with premium item companies are paid on commission, getting a job is not very difficult. You are assuming all of the risk. If you produce, everyone is happy and your career is under way.

WHERE THE JOBS ARE: Most major metropolitan areas have companies that specialize in premium sales.

KEYS TO GETTING THE JOB:
• Knowledge of merchandise and suppliers.
• Excellent communication skills.
• Good head for details.
• Aggressive personality.

PRINTING

POSITION: Printer

EDUCATION/TRAINING: Experience in printing process.

SALARY: Intro: $20,000
Average: $30,000
Top level: $100,000

JOB DESCRIPTION: To the surprise of many, printers are very involved in the business of sports. Think of how many things related to sports are printed on paper. Tickets. Season-ticket brochures. Souvenir programs. Baseball cards. Posters. Calendars. Yearbooks. Pocket schedules. Entry forms. Add to that all of the printed items a sports company needs to be in business, such as letterhead paper, envelopes, business cards, invoices, press kits, newsletter paper, and media guides. The list is huge. No wonder the companies specializing in sports printing do so well.

Jobs in printing run from the assistant to the printing press operator to general manager of the company. The jobs that allow for the most contact with sports are in sales, design/layout, and senior management.

Print salesmen are the company representatives who are out in the field generating business for the printer. Designers work in the print shop, making decisions with the client on how the particular job will look and what materials to use. And of course senior managers run the business. With printers who do a lot of sports business, it is very common to have very senior managers involved in the process every step of the way—not only because it's fun, but because the volume of business generated by a sports team, organization, or facility is not as likely to fluctuate from year to year as other accounts can. A steady revenue generator is a printer's dream. Plus, it adds prestige to the print shop and can be very profitable.

A typical sports print project works like this: the San Francisco Giants are thinking of producing 50,000 calendars to distribute to fans on opening day. They call ABC Printing to help them with the job.

ABC sends a sales representative and probably the general manager to the team's office to discuss the calendar. The Giants tell them how they want the calendar to look, how big it should be, how it folds, how it is stapled, how much color is going to be included, how many photos are going to be included, what kind of paper they want it printed on, who the sponsor is, and when they want it delivered. Armed with that information, ABC gives the Giants a price for the production and delivery of the calendars. Some negotiation takes place. To save money, the team decides to downgrade the quality of the paper a notch, and to use fewer photographs. Maybe it even throws in four season tickets and a luxury-suite night for ABC employees and customers to reduce the price. An agreement is reached.

It is at this point that the technical people take over. The artists and designers work with the Giants to select the pictures to be included in the calendar. They select the type style to use and the colors to include. They get all of the information the team wants in the calendar, like special giveaway nights, players' birthdays, ticket information, and, of course, game information. The designers take all of this input and make up the calendar. The team looks at it at stages along the way, making changes and giving approvals. Once the last approval is in, ABC prints and packages the calendars and ships them to Candlestick Park for distribution on opening day.

This process is repeated for each and every one of the printing projects the team has. Because the relationship is such a close one and the work requires so much contact, the printer develops a very strong tie with the team. And because consistency, meeting deadlines, and quality are so important to the team, it tends to stick with the same printer job in and job out.

Other opportunities in printing can be found in colleges across the country. Many of them have their own print shops to produce the tremendous volume of materials needed to run a college or university. Many of those orders come from the athletic department, for media guides, programs, tickets, brochures, and fliers. By showing an interest and expertise in working on these projects, you may be the one assigned to handle all of the sports printing tasks.

Still other jobs in printing can be found with companies that print materials on their own to sell to the general public. This includes companies that print things like baseball cards and posters. They obtain a licensing agreement or pay a rights fee for the photograph, then produce, distribute, and sell it at retail. Companies like Upper Deck and Topps have been tremendously successful with this kind of printing business.

Overall, the number of jobs in printing is very large. It takes many people to produce a complex piece of printed material. In terms of a career in sports, most of the jobs in printing do not apply. But by picking the right company with the right kind of sports products or clients, you may be able to build a career working in the sport and or with the team you love the most.

WHERE THE JOBS ARE: Independent print shops and printing companies across the U.S. Most of the ones with major sports printing business are located in sports cities.

KEYS TO GETTING THE JOB:
• Thorough familiarity with the process of printing.
• Ability to work with tight deadlines.
• Creativity.

PROMOTIONS

POSITION: Promotions director

EDUCATION/TRAINING: Degree in business, sports
administration.

SALARY: Intro: $25,000
Average: $40,000
Top level: $80,000

JOB DESCRIPTION: A sports promotions director is, obviously, responsible for promoting something, using sports as the tactic.

Different entities have different things they wish to promote. A corporation wants to promote its line of products. A facility wants to promote its use. A sports league wants to promote its teams and players. A radio station wants to promote its programming. A team wants to promote the excitement of its games. Even though the specifics of what these groups want to promote are different, they all turn to the promotions director to do the job.

Promotions directors run promotions. What is a promotion?

Loosely defined, a promotion is something of value that has been added to your product and that customers want. This promotional element is so valuable to customers, they will do something you want them to do in order to get it.

A common example is a giveaway at a baseball game. At a Cleveland Indians baseball game, the first 10,000 adult fans will receive a free wallet with their general-admission ticket. And in one hundred of those wallets will be a $50 bill. The Indians are counting on the fact that the wallet has a good perceived value, enough so that thousands of fans who don't normally go to games will be inclined to buy a ticket, and that some people who don't think the wallet itself is particularly valuable will come in hopes of winning the cash.

Another common example is radio station promotions. These can range from very simple come-ons, such as a ticket giveaway to the tenth caller, to elaborate schemes that require long periods of listening to claim a prize. Especially popular are the promotions that tell you, "Be listening between 7:00 and 7:15 Thursday morning to find out if you are the lucky winner." This is a strategic move by the station to boost its ratings, upon which most stations depend in order to raise their advertising rates.

Promotions come in all shapes and sizes and can have widely varying goals. In sports, the best promotions are usually built around some sort of media campaign. It isn't very effective if no one hears about it. The best ones are also the most simple, asking people to do just one or, at the most, two things. "Pick up your entry blank at the store, attach a proof of purchase, and mail it in."

The job of the promotions director is to identify the goal for the promotion, come up with a creative idea for the promotion, then execute the plan. Many sports groups have many different promotions going on at the same time. They may even differ based on what part of the country they are run in. In Minnesota they may be running a contest to win a free snowmobile, while at the same time of year in Arizona the prize is a round of golf with Arnold Palmer.

Jobs in promotion require an understanding of how people think about sports and products. They also take the ability to put value on intangible things like prestige and being "associated" with a star athlete. It helps to know how to make a multifaceted deal, where everyone chips in something and everyone gets something out of it. And of course, being able to manage a multitude of details is essential.

An example of a multipartner deal would be a three-way promotion between radio WXYZ, Northwest Airlines, and the Detroit Pistons. The idea is Instant Vacation Night. Go to the Pistons–Miami Heat game with your suitcase packed, dressed in Hawaiian clothing. A spotter from the station will pick out one lucky winner at the game. This person will be escorted to courtside seats, then after the game will be whisked to the airport by limousine to catch the late Northwest flight to Honolulu for a week's vacation, courtesy of Northwest, WXYZ, and the Pistons.

Each of the three partners benefits from this promotion. The radio station gets Northwest to buy an airtime schedule from it as part of the package. Northwest gets that airtime, it gets an equal amount of time free for participating in the contest, and it gets to highlight its service to Hawaii during the winter, when people are looking for someplace warm to go. And the team gets a slew of fans to show up for a game that would not otherwise have been a very big draw. Everyone shares in the fun idea, and the station and Northwest build a relationship with the team. Win-win-win for everyone.

Promotions positions can be excellent entry-level jobs. They include a good amount of responsibility, allow you to be creative, and offer good chances for advancement once you have gained some experience. Senior-level sales promotions directors are in demand, especially in these days of companies wanting more quantifiable results and questioning the effectiveness of media advertising.

Breaking into the sports promotions field can require obtaining some experience first. However, this is fairly easy to get by volunteering or working part-time for nonprofit companies and charities. Some of the best promotion work in the country is done on behalf of charities. Once you have this experience, getting a job with a team, league, facility, or sports company will be much easier.

WHERE THE JOBS ARE: Teams, leagues, facilities, sporting goods manufacturers, radio, television, newspapers, magazines, sports organizations, onetime events, colleges.

KEYS TO GETTING THE JOB:
• Creative promotional ideas.
• Experience in developing and executing promotions.
• Appropriate educational background.

PUBLIC-ADDRESS ANNOUNCER

POSITION: Public-address announcer

EDUCATION/TRAINING: No specific training needed.

SALARY: Intro: Paid per game
Average: $12,000
Top level: $25,000

JOB DESCRIPTION: The job of public-address announcer is almost always part-time, but it is one of the most unique and fun jobs in sports and is therefore included here.

The public-address announcer is the person who sits at the microphone in the stadium or arena and makes periodic announcements to the crowd over the speaker system. These announcements include information about the game or event ("Basket by MICH-ael JOR-dan"), information of a general nature ("Ladies and gentlemen, please remember that smoking is prohibited in the arena"), or commercial and promotional announcements ("Fans, remember that next Tuesday is Gatorade gym bag night").

Some events, such as golf tournaments, have little or no use for PA announcers; they announce the players at the first tee, and that's it. Others, like football games, use the announcer regularly to explain what has just happened or to identify who did what. And in some sports, like baseball and basketball, the PA announcer becomes part of the show.

For example, they way an announcer introduces the home team at a basketball game can build the crowd's excitement level to a fever pitch. The recap of a scoring play in hockey often gets more applause than the play itself. And sometimes announcers add to the enjoyment of a game just by virtue of the fact that because they have done it for so long and their voice is so distinctive, fans and players treat them as an important part of the big league experience.

The job of PA announcer requires a lot of preparation before the game or event. You need to make sure you can identify all of the athletes. You gather all of the copy for the announcement you need to make. In many cases, the announcements for the entire event arc prescripted. Every inning break, every time-out, the entire pregame and halftime—all are carefully pretimed and organized to make sure the information the public needs gets to them when it should. It is the job of the announcer to give it to them clearly, accurately, and, if possible, in an entertaining or at least nonoffensive way.

Salaries are typically low, again because most announcers work part-time or are paid per event. Many announcers also have other responsibilities with the team or facility, such as in sales or public relations. The real rewards come from being a part of the action, and knowing that what you are saying is being heard by thousands and thousands of fans every season.

WHERE THE JOBS ARE: Teams, facilities, and event promoters.

KEYS TO GETTING THE JOB:
• Strong, distinctive voice.
• Clear enunciation.
• Knowledge of the game and the athletes.
• A background in broadcasting, if possible.

PUBLIC RELATIONS

POSITIONS: Public relations manager

EDUCATION/TRAINING: Degree in public relations, communications, journalism.

SALARY: Intro: $12,000
Average: $30,000
Top level: $100,000

JOB DESCRIPTION: Public relations is an integral part of professional and collegiate sports. Every team, governing body, facility, organization, television network, and event has a public relations director. For the most part, the term "public relations" in sports is a misnomer. Public relations is a discipline that includes a lot of activities never seen in the world of sports. The public relations professional in sports is usually involved in two things: publicity and publications.

The thirst for information about athletes, teams, and coaches is unquenchable. The purveyors of information have so permeated the world of sports, participants now actually talk about what "the media" think and do. "He would have survived this losing streak okay, but the media got him." "The media didn't give us a chance in the series, and that got us pumped up enough to win." "The fans love me, but the media doesn't give me any respect." Managing this powerful publicity machine takes a lot of time and a good deal of expertise.

The task of generating publicity, of "getting ink," is one that all PR directors must be adept at. For most industries, this requires good contacts within the media and the ability to provide them with fresh story ideas or angles.

The process begins with a public relations plan. This plan contains the basic ideas you want the media to include in their stories and a time line to insure you get the most exposure possible for your team or event. The next step is to prepare the information materials you will distribute to the media, including press kits, press releases, photos, brochures, videotape, and samples. Once these have been prepared, they are sent or delivered to the media. This is then followed up with a phone call or letter, asking if they need more information or would like to arrange an interview. It is a very time-consuming process, but one that can be rewarded with a front-page story if things go right.

In some sports, however, this process is reversed, and turns into an exercise in time management. For example, on any given day Jerry Walker of the San Francisco 49ers could get requests from ten people in the media who want to talk with Joe Montana. Joe can't talk with ten—he would be there all night. So Jerry manages the requests. He favors the larger media outlets, giving first shot to network television, the *New York Times, Sports Illustrated*—the majors. He then categorizes the other requests. His hometown newspapers are certainly a priority, but perhaps today he can get them to focus on another player. They are there every day; they can talk to Joe another time. Other requests may be from a small-town newspaper or a radio station outside the market. This station, say, doesn't cover the team regularly and never sends a representative to a game, but someone came up with the thought this morning that it would be great if the station could do an exclusive feature on Joe. Jerry may try to get it to do something with another player. If that doesn't work, he'll deny its request for an in-person interview, but invite it to participate in one of Joe's weekly conference calls.

In the end, Joe does two quick television interviews, sits down with one writer for fifteen minutes, and leaves. Joe is happy knowing that he has done his public relations duty for the team that day and doesn't feel overused or that his time was wasted, and Jerry has managed to generate not only the three stories on Joe, but four more on other players who were originally second choices. The other media outlets will be disappointed, but have left with a clearer understanding of the policies and practices of the 49ers and will take advantage of the conference call to get what they need.

This example shows how the publicity process for professional teams and events can turn around. Suddenly, you aren't worrying about getting media attention, but instead are wondering how you can squeeze it all in and still keep everyone happy, and with fresh stories and angles.

The second major responsibility for the public relations department is in the area of publications. This runs the gamut from writing and distributing daily press releases to producing hundred-page, multicolor media guides, souvenir programs, and yearbooks. These projects require good writing skills and a thorough knowledge of the printing industry. They also require expertise in working with computers and desktop publishing.

Public relations departments with teams are commonly composed of two to four people. At facilities, racetracks, and events, the staff may be smaller than that; large corporations, televisions networks, and agencies may be somewhat larger. Even though the size of staffs are small, since virtually every sports group has at least one PR person the overall number of jobs available is quite large.

The compensation for PR jobs in sports is usually lower than in other industries, the amount of time spent on the job is much higher, and the amount of recognition you receive for your efforts is practically nil. Despite these drawbacks, public relations jobs in sports remain some of the most coveted.

If you ask a sports public relations person what he or she does for a living, you may get a variety of answers. The real answer is that they talk on the telephone, setting up interviews and pitching story ideas, and they write, generating game notes, press releases, and player bios by the score. Those two activities take up seventy-five percent of the day. The other part is spent talking in person with athletes, reporters, and writers, making sure that the media gets what they need and that the players' time isn't abused and they aren't taken advantage of. The final, most insignificant part of the job is actually sitting down and watching games or events. So when someone tells you he has a friend in sports PR who gets paid for just sitting in the press box, eating food, and watching games, you'll know the rest of the story.

To get a job in sports PR begins in school. You must be an

HOW TO GET A JOB IN SPORTS

excellent writer in order to do this job. Virtually every PR person in sports has some sort of college degree, frequently in journalism. A good way to begin your career is by working in your college's sports information department. This will give you an idea of what kind of things the press is looking for, what makes a good story, and how to work with athletes. Once you have graduated, there are a large number of individual events you will be able to work on to get experience, such as local softball championships and auto races. Take every opportunity to write you can get, keep getting involved in all of the events and with all of the teams you can as a helper or a stringer for a media outlet, and if you show some ability you will soon be a candidate for a job in sports public relations.

WHERE THE JOBS ARE: All professional sports teams, leagues, facilities, colleges, major media outlets, professional and amateur associations, manufacturers, sponsoring corporations, government sports bodies.

KEYS TO GETTING THE JOB:
• Excellent writing ability.
• Familiarity with printing industry.
• Desktop publishing skills, if possible.
• Thorough knowledge of the sport.
• Ability to come up with creative story ideas.
• Good networking and relationship-building skills.

PUBLISHING

POSITION: Book publishing, editorial

EDUCATION/TRAINING: Degree in journalism, publishing.

SALARY: Intro: $16,000
Average: $50,000
Top level: $100,000

JOB DESCRIPTION: The publishing of sports books is a billion-dollar industry in the United States alone. Most of the books published fall into four categories: the athlete biography, "how-to" books, information/fact books, or histories.

The athlete biography typically is a ghostwritten or cowritten biography of a person who is still living and who has achieved greatness or at least notoriety in his or her sport. Most of the great sports stars of the past fifty years have had their lives chronicled in one form of sports biography or another.

How-to books offer tips in self-improvement, from getting thinner thighs to hitting your three wood ten yards farther. They are heavily weighted in the area of individual performance, but also include books on how to coach sports and on different team strategies. These are for the most part written by people with real or implied expertise in the area, such as a book by Jack Nicklaus on how to play golf or by Arnold Schwarzenegger on bodybuilding techniques.

Information/fact books lay out the facts and figures for fans to study and enjoy. Books in this category include the sports almanacs, Bill James's statistical abstracts, and the *Baseball Encyclopedia*. These books are mostly compilations of what has happened statistically in a sport, and sometimes include an analysis of the facts and figures by the author.

Histories may have as subjects such things as great football rivalries, basketball in the ACC, or specific individuals who have had an influence on sports, like Red Grange or Babe Ruth. Histories differ from player biographies in that they are usually more scholarly in nature, trying to put the athlete and his accomplishments in some kind of historical prospective instead of just recounting the events of his or her life in chronological order.

Jobs in publishing relate to the acquisition of the rights to publish these books; supervision of the writing, editing, and production of the book; management of its distribution, advertising, and publicity; and, of course, the handling of all of the financial considerations involved, such as contract negotiations and royalty payments.

All books get started with an idea. The idea can come from anywhere—a writer, an agent, an athlete, an editor, you name it. It is the job of the sports book editor to sort through these ideas and come up with the ones that will sell the most books. Editors must stay on top of what is happening in the world of sports, to make sure they get a chance to be involved in the best book projects.

Getting a job in sports book publishing starts with a degree in English or journalism. In many cases, editors are graduates of specific book-publishing programs, such as those offered at Radcliffe or Denver. Since sports book publishing is a fairly narrow field, most editors start out working with other kinds of books and then develop their specialty in sports. Entry-level jobs usually fall under the title of editorial assistant. These jobs are available to top graduates directly out of school. From there, you can guide your career based on your interests and available opportunities.

WHERE THE JOBS ARE: Major publishing centers such as New York City, Chicago, and Los Angeles.

KEYS TO GETTING THE JOB:
• Strong college education
• Degree in publishing/journalism/English
• Previous internship
• Start in a small publishing house or university press

POSITION: Magazine publishing

EDUCATION/TRAINING: Degree in journalism, publishing.

SALARY: Intro: $20,000
         Average: $40,000
         Top level: $200,000

JOB DESCRIPTION: Sports magazines come in all shapes and sizes, from the national sports news publications like *Sports Illustrated* to monthly special-interest magazines like *San Francisco Citysports*. They are different in some ways, such as budgets and staff size, but in the most important ways they are exactly the same. They each offer opportunities in three main job areas: production, distribution, and advertising sales.

Production refers to the process required to put the publication together, assembling the contributions of writers, editors, and photographers on a deadline into the best format possible. Production jobs include jobs in writing, editing, and photography, as well as the print production jobs such as doing color separations or layouts and running printing presses. In smaller operations, one person often does more than one job.

Distribution handles getting the publication into people's hands, by mailing it to them directly or providing copies to stores where they can buy it. Distribution jobs include generating subscriptions, working with retail outlets and brokerage houses to make the magazine available at retail, and distributing it at special events. The job is crucial to the success of the magazine, not only because of the amount of revenue that can be generated from individual copy sales, but because increasing the number of people who read the magazine allows you to charge more for advertising space within it.

Once an audience is established, **advertising sales** sells space to companies interested in reaching that audience. Sales is the department that generates the bulk of the revenue for any sports magazine. Salespeople are on the telephone and in offices calling on potential customers every day, describing the benefits of advertising in their publication. Of all the jobs in publishing, sales jobs are the ones that involve the most contact outside the company. They also tend to pay the best. Most salespeople are paid on a commission, which means that they receive a percentage of every ad dollar they generate. Successful salesmen for large national magazines routinely earn $100,000 or more every year.

Jobs in magazine publishing are fairly easy to get if you have the proper academic background and a strong interest in a particular sport. There are, after all, hundreds of sports magazines published around the country. The vast majority of them are quite small, with limited audiences. This in turn limits your earning potential. But, if you are a skilled writer, editor, or salesperson with an interest in sports, chances are good that you will be able to land a job in magazine publishing. And once you are in the field and have gotten some experience, it is easier to move up to better and better jobs.

WHERE THE JOBS ARE: Most major cities across the country have one or more sports magazine publishers. Large, national magazines are often headquartered in New York City.

KEYS TO GETTING THE JOB:
• Educational background in journalism, publishing.
• Sales experience.
• Willingness to start at a small regional publication to learn the trade.

RADIO

POSITION: Broadcaster

EDUCATION/TRAINING: Degree in broadcast journalism.

SALARY: Intro: $15,000
Average: $30,000
Top level: $500,000 plus

JOB DESCRIPTION: Radio sports broadcasters are for many people the link between the sport and the fan. Radio is very accessible and affordable, enabling just about everyone to be able to listen to his favorite team or event. The broadcasters, especially the play-by-play announcers, become an extension of the team. Vin Scully and the Dodgers, Chick Hearn and the Lakers, and Johnny Most and the Celtics are examples of how tight the association between radio personalities and teams can become.

Jobs in sports radio broadcasting originate from two sources. You may either work for a radio broadcaster, such as a station or a network, or you may work directly for a sports promoter, such as a team or special event. In college sports and professional football, the game announcers work for a radio station. In baseball, basketball, and hockey the situation varies, with many announcers working directly for the team. The broadcast of major events, such as the Super Bowl, World Series, and Indianapolis 500, is contracted through a radio network, often with the selection of the announcers stipulated in the contract.

Besides play-by-play, radio sports broadcasting takes two other forms: it is either part of the regular news-gathering and reporting function of a station, or it is part of the station's entertainment programming.

On the news side, the sports reporter is part of the hourly news-sports-weather-traffic information block. It includes reading sports scores, breaking sports news stories of the day from the wire services, interviewing local sports figures, and doing special features and editorials, all within the format of the station. Most stations with a news talk format, especially AM stations in larger markets, have at least one full-time sports personality on the air.

Sports as programming usually takes the form of a hosted call-in show for fans. The host will have sports celebrities in the studio or on the telephone, and fans may call in and ask them questions. The sports call-in show is becoming more and more popular around the country, as stations struggle to compete with television in the evening hours.

The radio broadcasting business is highly competitive for top jobs. Unlike television, where appearances count, in radio a good voice and the ability to do the job are all that matter. Most radio sports broadcasters these days get their start in college, at a school that offers them the chance to be on the air while they learn about the business. They then move to small stations in the hinterlands to get some experience. From there they change jobs as opportunities arise, always moving to larger and larger stations in bigger and bigger markets, until they eventually get their chance at the big time. In fact, most of the big names in television—people like Al Michaels, Bob Costas, and Vin Scully—started their careers in radio.

The important things to do to start a career in radio sports are to gain technical mastery of the equipment, to get some background education in writing and journalism, and to keep working at it. Take a tape recorder to games and simulate doing the play-by-play. Then listen to your tape and work on improving it. Also, remember that local stations and even national radio networks can't afford to have someone at every event, even every big one. It is often easy to get jobs with local stations or networks on a free-lance basis, going into locker rooms (with station credentials) and getting quotes on tape for them to play over the air. Your voice may not be heard, but you will get experience in asking questions and learning how to probe to get something interesting on tape. If your tape is used on the air, you will even get paid for your effort.

In the end, getting a job in sports broadcasting boils down to how professional and appealing you sound on the air and whether the program director at the station or the team's director of broadcasting likes what you do. The more work you do to improve, the better your chances of success will be.

WHERE THE JOBS ARE: Radio stations across the country; radio networks, based primarily in New York City; professional sports teams.

KEYS TO GETTING THE JOB:
• Good voice.
• Educational background in broadcasting, journalism.
• As much experience as you can get: working as a student, free-lancing, interning at stations, or doing the midnight-6:00 A.M. shift at a local station.
• Sports knowledge.

POSITION: Broadcast producer

EDUCATION/TRAINING: Degree in broadcast journalism.

SALARY: Intro: $15,000
Average: $25,000
Top level: $100,000

JOB DESCRIPTION: The radio producer is the person who puts together all of the elements of the sports broadcast to form a complete show. The producer formats the broadcast, creating a document that shows where the taped features go and where and how long the commercial breaks are, and sets up interviews or news reports for halftime or between periods. He works with radio stations along the affiliate network, making sure their needs are being met. The producer works with the engineer to make sure all lines and satellite feeds are in place for remote broadcasts, and makes sure all of the commercials, promotional announcements, and public-service spots are included in the broadcast. In short, the producer is responsible for the overall sound of the show, from the opening theme music to the closing billboards.

Producing an in-studio sports show also includes booking the guests, getting their background information for the announcer, and promoting the show during other parts of the day. It may also mean doing some publicity for the show, such as calling newspapers on a weekly or daily basis to let them know the guest lineup.

Sports call-in show producers are highly organized and energetic. Good ones have contacts all over the country—their most valued possession is their Rolodex and its private phone numbers. It's 7:15 and Bo Jackson has canceled. Maybe you can get Jose Canseco to do a phone interview if you can reach him in his car. It is a hectic, often thankless, behind-the-scenes job, but it can also be one of the most fun jobs in sports. What other job would enable you to talk with Mickey Mantle, John Elway, Mario Andretti, Tom Watson, and Carl Lewis in the same week?

Getting a job as a radio producer starts with education. You must be familiar with all of the equipment used to put a broadcast over the air, be adept at editing tape, and be able to operate the control board during the broadcast. This kind of expertise only comes with experience. The best way to get this kind of experience is to work at a radio station. Get a job at your college station or at a small station outside of town, or do an internship at a large station. Most producers working in sports today started at small stations somewhere and worked their way up, just like broadcasters. The skills needed to get a quality broadcast on the air in Mendocino, California, are the same ones you need to broadcast the Yankees game in New York.

WHERE THE JOBS ARE: Mainly AM stations in medium to large radio markets.

KEYS TO GETTING THE JOB:
• Technical expertise in all phases of broadcasting.
• Organization skills.

- Good contacts in the world of sports.
- Creativity.

POSITION: Engineer

EDUCATION/TRAINING: Degree in electronics; FCC license; some stations require union membership.

SALARY: Intro: $18,000
Average: $30,000
Top level: $75,000

JOB DESCRIPTION: The engineer at a radio station is the person in charge of maintaining the signal on the air. The job requires some expertise in a wide variety of sciences, including electronics, acoustics, and audio engineering. It includes working with the signal from its origination point at a ballpark, through the radio station to the signal tower, and out over the air to the fans.

Of course, engineers are involved in sports broadcasting in the same way they are involved in all broadcasting—without their help, the station would be silent. However, they often are involved in sports more directly, by setting up and managing remote broadcasts.

If you listen to the credits at the end of a remote radio broadcast, you will hear the announcer thank his engineer. At a remote location, the engineer is the person who sets up and maintains the broadcast equipment. He builds, in effect, a mobile radio station, and is responsible for keeping the announcers on the air and the sound quality high. He shifts the sound from the announcers' booth to the crowd microphone during a particularly exciting play, or patches in another reporter to give a report from the sideline. Often, the engineer is required to insert the commercials at the appropriate time or is in contact with a person at the station who plugs them in. He even cues the announcers, helping them with promotional announcements and commercials that are read live on the air.

Remote engineers must be technical experts. They first have to plan the broadcast and decide what kind of equipment setup they will need to accomplish the job. Then, if something goes wrong, they have to be able to diagnose and fix it in split seconds. They have to know how to protect the equipment in any weather, from snowstorms to heat waves. And they have to be calm under pressure, able to adjust to the unexpected and deal accordingly.

Just as with many other jobs in radio, becoming an engineer starts with getting the proper education. Once you have built up the technical knowledge you need, get a job with a radio station somewhere—any station, anywhere. They all send up signals, and you will be able to learn more by working on the equipment firsthand than you would in any class. Some stations, particularly those in the largest markets, have substantial engineering staffs. At these stations, you may be able to find part-time work on weekends or evenings, or as a vacation fill-in, enabling you to get your feet wet on the job and still have some supervision. Being an engineer is somewhat unusual in that the pressure doesn't come when you have a problem at noon on a weekday. There are a lot of people around to pitch in and help then. The pressure comes when you have a breakdown at 3:00 A.M. Christmas Day, and the only person available to prevent the signal from turning into hours of dead air is you. At these times, you will be thankful for all the time you spent at that little station in the boondocks that had this kind of problem every month.

WHERE THE JOBS ARE: Every radio station in the country has at least one engineer; some have as many as ten or more on a full- or part-time basis.

KEYS TO GETTING THE JOB:
• Technical expertise.
• FCC license.
• Union membership (if required).

POSITION: Promotions

EDUCATION/TRAINING: Degree in marketing, advertising, public relations.

SALARY: Intro: $15,000
               Average: $25,000
               Top level: $70,000

JOB DESCRIPTION: The promotions director at a team flagship radio station is charged with helping the station take full advantage of its special status.

The first job is to let as many people as possible know that the station is carrying the games. This is done in a variety of ways, from promotional announcements on the air to publicity to advertising. The goal is to build the audience, improving the ratings not only during the game broadcast but also during other parts of the day. It is widely believed that being one of the five set dial positions on a car radio is the key to radio ratings success. By being the station of the Broncos, or the Bulls, or the Redskins, your station is a likely place for a button to be set. Once you are in that position, people are likely to sample your station during other parts of the day as well as during the games.

The second part of the promotions director's responsibility is to work with the sales department in putting together advertising packages. A large in-game sponsor may receive two season tickets and a trip to an away game as part of the advertising buy. If tickets are hard to get, this may be just the thing to get it to buy a sponsorship package. It is up to the promotions director to devise these programs and then carry them out.

The third part of a promotions director's job comes under the area of public service or listener relations. This includes things such as ticket giveaways, listener-appreciation tailgate parties, and promoting the charity canned-food drive at the upcoming game. These are things the station does to reward its loyal listeners, to keep building the relationship between the listener and the station, and to show that the station and the team are community-oriented.

The promotions director's job requires a good working relationship with the teams that are his or her broadcast partners, a strong list of contacts within the community, expertise in sales promotion, public relations, and advertising, and the creativity needed to come up with new and different programs from client to client and season to season. This kind of experience can come from a variety of jobs, such as working for nonprofit organizations putting together promotions, or being a junior-level account executive in a marketing, advertising, or public relations firm.

Good promotions directors at top-level stations in large markets have a great deal of experience and expertise. But, small stations, stations in small markets, and stations doing poorly in the ratings need to do promotions, too. These are the kinds of stations that will hire someone with less experience, and here are the entry-level jobs you should seek out.

WHERE THE JOBS ARE: Flagship radio stations, major sports team network affiliate stations.

KEYS TO GETTING THE JOB:
• Background in sales or promotion.
• Good contacts within the community.
• Broad sports knowledge and interest.
• Creative promotional ideas.

POSITION: Sales

EDUCATION/TRAINING: Sales training or experience helpful but not required.

SALARY: Intro: $18,000
                 Average: $35,000
                 Top level: $100,000 plus

JOB DESCRIPTION: Radio sports sales has become something of a specialty in the radio business. At stations with contracts to broadcast play-by-play, or which include sports as a significant part of their programming, the sales staff usually includes some people with a special interest or expertise in sports sales.

The radio salesperson sells commercial advertising broadcast time in thirty-second or one-minute intervals. The clients then use that time to air their commercials. Because sports programming usually attracts a very large audience, the cost of these commercials is much higher than the cost of regular time on the station. That in turn leads to higher salaries for the sales staff, who are paid a commission on what they sell. The success or failure of the sales effort often depends on what kind of overall marketing package can be built around the sponsorship, including such things as tickets, luxury boxes, nights at the game for employees, and appearances by players.

Selling radio time can be a very lucrative profession, with top salespeople in major markets earning over $100,000 per year.

Getting a job in radio sports sales starts with working for the right station. A station playing classical music will not allow you the chance to get the kind of packaging experience you will need to become a good sports salesperson. It is preferable to work in AM radio, which is much more news-and-information-oriented. This will require you to have some creativity in putting together packages for sponsors, just as you will with sports sales. It is also likely that your station will carry some sports, especially in smaller markets, which is good preparation too. Stations are always on the lookout for salespeople, so getting a job in this area should not be difficult if you meet the minimum qualifications, which in most cases include a college degree, some retail sales experience, and a professional appearance. Once you have some success stories under your belt, keep your eyes open for opportunities to work for the big play-by-play broadcaster in your area. Talk with the sales manager and let him or her know you are interested. If the sales manager thinks you can make money for the station, you will soon have a job in radio sports sales.

WHERE THE JOBS ARE: Radio stations that carry sports play-by-play, either as flagship or network affiliate.

KEYS TO GETTING THE JOB:
• Well-developed sales skills.
• Good knowledge and enthusiasm about sports.

RESTAURANT MANAGEMENT

POSITION: Sports restaurant management

EDUCATION/TRAINING: Degree in restaurant management preferred.

Salary: Intro: $18,000
Average: $30,000
Top level: $60,000

JOB DESCRIPTION: The sports bar and restaurant now has a permanent place in American society. Years ago, a sports bar was someplace like Toots Shor's in New York, where athletes, promoters, reporters, and others associated with sports hung out, enjoyed a beer or two, and talked sports. With the advent of television, the sports-bar concept evolved to include places where the average fan would go to watch a fight or a ball game on TV. Technological advances moved the concept even further ahead. Big-screen, rear-projection televisions allowed whole roomfuls of fans to watch sporting events like Monday Night Football, giving the sports bar the same kind of feeling of excitement as you would get at the event itself—complete with waitress service, easy parking, and nearby bathrooms, I might add. The "Urban Cowboy" craze carried it a bit further, proving you could fill a restaurant with bull-riding machines, punching bags, and other games and machines and attract a crowd night after night.

Today, some of the most elaborate sports facilities in the country are sports restaurants. They have many large-screen televisions hooked up to their own satellite dishes, enabling them to get multiple games from different parts of the country at the same time. They have video games, basketball hoops, auto-racing simulators, batting cages, even places where you can tee up a golf ball and pretend you are playing the eighteenth hole at Pebble Beach.

While not directly tied to sports, these restaurants offer the opportunity to be immersed in the world of sports from morning till night. The biggest ones, or the ones in major sports cities, are frequented by athletes, coaches, and sports personalities just as Toots Shor's was years ago. They host a series of special events, including autograph sessions with athletes, remote radio broadcasts of sports talk shows, and parties for every season: college bowl game parties, NBA draft parties, World Series parties, and the biggest of them all, the Super Bowl Party. Sports memorabilia lines the walls, the sports page is behind the bar, and if you want to you can usually place a friendly wager with someone on the outcome of the next game.

Jobs in sports restaurant management include the usual challenges of food preparation and service, staffing, and marketing. The first two are the same in any restaurant. The goals are to feature quality food and beverages, prepared and served by a professional staff, that generate as much profit as possible. It is the marketing of the bar or restaurant that involves the manager in sports, organizing bus trips to the ball game for opening day and pools for the Final Four.

To get a job in sports restaurant management takes either a degree in restaurant management or some restaurant management experience. Particularly valuable would be experience in a high-volume restaurant with a good bar business that has a lot of young adults as customers. Then seek out the opportunities in your area, either with an existing sports restaurant or with one that would be willing to let you convert it to the sports-bar concept.

Restaurant management is a job that includes long hours, many staffing headaches, and a lot of hard work. But if you love sports, managing a sports restaurant can be a lot of fun. And in many ways, you can be more involved in a wider variety of sports than the people actually working for teams, leagues, and events.

WHERE THE JOBS ARE: Major young-adult-oriented chain restaurants, independent sports bars and restaurants.

KEYS TO GETTING THE JOB:
• Degree in restaurant management.
• Restaurant management experience.
• Willingness to work long hours, nights, and weekends.

RETAIL SALES

POSITION: Sports theme stores

EDUCATION/TRAINING: Retail sales experience.

SALARY: Intro: $18,000
Average: $25,000
Top level: $70,000

JOB DESCRIPTION: Jobs working in sporting goods stores are, of course, an obvious way to get involved in sports. However, some unique kinds of retail stores are opening across the country that enable you to get involved in professional sports in a much more direct way. These are the sports theme stores.

In San Francisco, the Giants have for years run stores they call Giants Dugout Stores. There you can buy all sorts of souvenirs from the team, as well as from other teams in baseball and other sports. They have a wide variety of hats, shirts, jackets, and other items. They carry things one step further, however, in that you can also buy Giants tickets there and special one-of-a-kind items like broken baseball bats and autographed balls. It is the best way for a fan to interact with the team without going to Candlestick Park.

Many clubs in baseball and in other sports have picked up on the success of the Giants and opened their own retail outlets. Others have contracted with independent management companies to run their stores for them.

More and more of these sports theme stores are springing up around the country. Teams, leagues, and associations license merchandise, which is then distributed to the retail outlet for sale. These retail stores do a great business, in all kinds of logo- or team-identified merchandise, and in the area of collectibles with such items as cards and autographs.

A job in a retail sports theme store, working for a team, association, or licensee, gives you the opportunity to surround yourself with sports memorabilia all day long. It also enables you to interact with sports fans one on one, helping them buy something that shows their support for a team, sport, or individual or that adds to their collection.

Of course, the nuts and bolts of retailing govern the business. Things like location of the store, inventory management, and customer service are still the keys to success. But by being involved in a business that requires you to be somewhat knowledgeable about sports, and that enables you to talk about sports with virtually every customer, you may find yourself anxious to get to work every day.

WHERE THE JOBS ARE: Selected major league teams, sporting goods and sports memorabilia chains and independent stores.

KEYS TO GETTING THE JOB:
• Background in retailing, if possible.
• Professional appearance.
• Enthusiasm for sports and the merchandise.

RODEO

POSITION: Professional rodeo management

EDUCATION/TRAINING: No specific background required.

SALARY: Intro: $12,000
Average: $20,000
Top level: $100,000

JOB DESCRIPTION: Jobs in rodeo are almost all done on a contract basis, from event to event. Rodeo workers fall into three categories: those who travel from event to event, those who work on one event only, and those who work for the Professional Rodeo Cowboys Association in Colorado Springs.

The rodeo circuit is no different from the professional golf or the professional tennis circuit. The show moves from city to city each week, and the athletes, officials, and much of the administrative staff move with them. The difference is, in the same weekend there may be five rodeos in five different states. (The best cowboys will try to make three of them, even if it means they have to drive all night to do it.) Professional rodeo workers contract with events individually, trying to string them together in such a way as to minimize their expenses and maximize their revenue. In that way, it is possible to earn a pretty good living by rodeoing year round.

Examples of the kind of jobs available on the rodeo circuit include public-address announcer, bullfighter, and judge.

The public-address announcer at a rodeo will probably be the highest-paid person there. The announcer is crucial to the success of the event. It is the announcer who keeps the rodeo action flowing, explains the events, and keeps the audience involved and entertained. Top announcers demand top dollar, earning as much as $100,000 in the course of a year.

Bullfighters are the men dressed as clowns whose job it is to distract the bulls when cowboys are bucked off, to enable them to get to safety. They do this in a variety of ways, most often by just catching the bull's eye and leading him away from the cowboy. It takes quickness, strength, and stamina, and a good deal of knowledge about how a bull moves and reacts. Good bullfighters are in high demand on the circuit. Everyone wants the cowboys to be as protected as possible. A good bullfighter can make over $50,000 per year.

Rodeo judges and officials are usually affiliated with the PRCA. This insures they have received some training at a PRCA school, in an effort to make the judging from event to event more even. They are the people who judge the quality of the livestock and the quality of the cowboy's ride, the two elements that make up the overall score. Rodeo judges earn as much as $40,000 per year.

Full-time jobs with single events are uncommon. Even the largest rodeos are managed by part-time staff members, and the majority of them are volunteers.

To get a full-time position in rodeo starts with working part-time. This means getting involved with the PRCA on a local level, helping put on individual rodeos in your area, working for a livestock contractor, and in general being around the sport. It is a small, fairly closed community. By showing some interest in the rodeo and having the capability to move from city to city, you will soon be able to try just about every job there is to be had in the business. Once you have found one you like, take the necessary steps to be among the best in the country at it and you will be on your way to a career in rodeo.

WHERE THE JOBS ARE: Livestock contractors, PRCA in Colorado Springs.

KEYS TO GETTING THE JOB:
• Experience in working with livestock, especially horses.
• Good physical condition (bullfighting).
• Experience in radio (announcer).
• Willingness to travel.

SALES

POSITION: Sports sales

EDUCATION/TRAINING: Sales experience preferred.

SALARY: Intro: $12,000
Average: $35,000
Top level: $250,000

JOB DESCRIPTION: Many of the jobs in sports revolve around sales. Franchises are sold to owners. Tickets are sold to fans. Television time is sold to advertisers. If a person has developed skills in the area of sales, there is a place for him or her in the world of sports.

To the surprise of many non-salespeople, selling is a skill. There is no such thing as a "natural-born salesman." There are people who have natural abilities in listening, speaking, and persuasion, but these are talents that can also be learned. The best salespeople are those who study the art of selling and who work at improving their skills all the time.

Sales jobs in sports are not only relatively large in number, but they are also the easiest jobs in sports to get, because the salesperson assumes all of the risk. If you are working on a commission basis, you only get paid if you produce. And if you can produce, there will always be a job for you.

The list of sports sales jobs is virtually endless. Some of them are very specialized, such as the sale of artificial turf to outdoor stadiums. Others are broad, such as selling tickets or advertising. To see what kind of sales jobs might be available in the area you want to work, do some research. What businesses exist there? How do they generate revenue? Who are their customers? Who is selling what to whom? What is being sold—products, services, entertainment, something else? By doing your homework, you may be able to find a specific need that your sales skills can fill or uncover a job opportunity that you never knew existed.

As an example, take professional golf. A tournament comes to town every year, which you have attended faithfully for the last few years. You would love to use your sales skills to get involved, but how?

Next time you go to a golf event, take a look around. There is a large area with tents set up for corporate entertainment. There is obviously some selling going on in there. And someone had to sell the tent space and catering to the corporate sponsors. Notice all of the signage at the golf course. If these companies bought it, someone must be in charge of selling it to them. The same with all of the ads in the souvenir program. Of course, someone must be in charge of selling all of the tickets to the event.

A closer look at the program gives you your answer. In the tournament staff directory is listed a director of sales. "One person to do all of this? I wonder if some opportunities are being missed from a lack of manpower." You contact the director of sales and discover he could desperately use some help in selling corporate sponsorships and tickets, but has little budget to pay a person to do it. But by working out a commission arrangement, you get the kind of compensation you need and the tournament gets added revenue for the next year's tournament.

This example is hypothetical, but it is a reflection of the power a good salesperson has in the sports business marketplace. If you have enough credibility to get in the door and the necessary skills to do the job, more often than not you will be given the chance to succeed or fail as a sports salesperson.

Compensation in sales is totally dependent on what you are selling and how well you sell it. In that sense, the earning potential is only limited by your goals and expertise.

Sales careers in sports can be among the most exciting and dynamic in the industry. The job is always changing, always moving forward, always challenging. While not for the timid or weak of heart, selling is often the best job in an organization in terms of security, earning potential, and, most important of all, the amount of fun you can have.

WHERE THE JOBS ARE: Teams, leagues, corporations, sports organizations, media, signage companies, sporting goods manufacturers, agencies.

KEYS TO GETTING THE JOB:
• Knowledge of the product, whether it is a particular sport, a piece of equipment, or a line of services.
• Ability to sell.
• Professional appearance.

SCOREBOARD OPERATOR

POSITION: Scoreboard operator

EDUCATION/TRAINING: Some electronics training.

SALARY: Intro: Paid per game
Average: $20,000
Top level: $35,000

JOB DESCRIPTION: The job of operating the scoreboard at a facility or for a team used to be strictly a volunteer job or one that paid a small amount of money per game. The building of the spectacular scoreboard at the Houston Astrodome, complete with graphics and fireworks, changed all that. Now most buildings have scoreboards with graphics capabilities. Many have giant television screens as well, for replays, preproduced game highlights, and features. All of this technology has added a great deal to the fans' enjoyment of the game. It has also upgraded the position of scoreboard operator.

The typical control booth for today's scoreboard operator resembles a television studio. From that location, a staff of people operate all of the scoreboards, run the giant replay screen, and control such other elements as the music and public-address announcements. They may be monitoring other games on satellite, and showing replays of these games on the big screen during time-outs. They orchestrate the game, trying to maintain excitement by showing a good play on replay or by playing upbeat music when a rally is needed. It has gone far beyond the simple job of keeping score. The scoreboard is a part of the whole entertainment package, and the scoreboard operator is at the controls.

Getting a job as a scoreboard operator starts with experience or a degree in television production. This will enable you to work with the broadcast department of any facility in the country, no matter how sophisticated its scoreboard is. Many teams have seasonal positions in this area, giving you an opportunity to learn on the job part-time, as an intern, or as a volunteer. Baseball teams are especially likely to have entry-level positions in this area.

WHERE THE JOBS ARE: Sports facilities built in the last twenty years, or where scoreboards have been updated.

KEYS TO GETTING THE JOB:
• Knowledge of television production.
• Creative ideas about music and video selection.
• Willingness to start as a game-day volunteer to learn how the equipment works.

SCOUTING

POSITION: Scouting

EDUCATION/TRAINING: Playing, coaching, or scouting experience.

SALARY: Intro: $25,000
Average: $35,000
Top level: $100,000

JOB DESCRIPTION: Scouting refers to looking at and evaluating the players in a particular sport to determine their ability to play in the professional league.

Most teams in all of the major leagues have staff positions devoted to the scouting of colleges in the U.S. and Canada to identify and evaluate players who may be able to help the big league club. In baseball and hockey, scouts look at players even younger than that, sometimes evaluating them as early as junior high school. And in sports like football and basketball, the league is involved in scouting as well, helping the teams identify and rate players so that they are all on a more equal footing come draft day.

Scouts travel extensively, watching players in games during the season or during practice, talking with coaches, gathering and looking at film of past performances, and talking with players. They may work out of a team office or out of their own office, which is usually their home. Many teams break up the country into regions and assign one scout to a particular region. While this cuts down the long-distance travel considerably, it still is a job that takes you away from home a great deal of the time.

A typical week for a baseball scout might include watching as many as seven high school, junior college, or college games in seven different towns. During each game, he takes notes on the players he is interested in and tries to pick up things on other up-and-coming players as well. He may talk with several coaches and managers, look at some videotape, and talk with people in the community, such as former major league players, to try to get an idea of a kid's ability. It is a lot of motel rooms, rental cars, and fast food, but if you find a couple of Major Leaguers, an All-Star, and a future Hall of Famer, it is all worth it.

Jobs in scouting almost always go to former players or coaches. The best way to break into the field is to work on a part-time basis. For example, you may offer to scout a small-college basketball tournament during the holidays to keep track of a particular player for a team. In football, help is always needed in breaking down film and evaluating college players. The most important ingredient is to win the trust of the scouting director, to show him that you are able to identify what it takes to play in the big leagues and that you are consistent in your evaluations. If you can do this, you will be able to get a job as a scout.

WHERE THE JOBS ARE: Major sports franchises, combines, league scouting services.

KEYS TO GETTING THE JOB:
- Playing, coaching, or scouting experience on college or professional level.
- Willingness to travel for long periods of time.
- Ability to interact with a wide variety of people, from eighteen-year-old players to sixty-year-old coaches.

SECRETARY

POSITION: Secretary

EDUCATION/TRAINING: Word processing, typing.

SALARY: Intro: $15,000
Average: $25,000
Top level: $45,000

JOB DESCRIPTION: Even by any other name—administrative assistant, coordinator, word processor, and so on—the job of secretary has lost its luster. It is perceived, probably correctly so, as a dead-end job. If you do it poorly, you are fired; if you do it well, your boss is so grateful that it would take an act of Congress to enable you to change jobs within the company. It can be thankless, with long hours and low pay.

Given all of this, the simple fact remains that every sports organization has secretaries on staff. The New York Giants, the Boston Celtics, Madison Square Garden, ABC Sports, the Indianapolis Motor Speedway, the Louisiana Superdome—every sports group or organization has a need for secretarial support. It is the one job category that exists across the board. If you want to get a job in sports, don't ignore the idea of becoming a secretary.

While advancement is rare, some of today's sports executives started their careers as secretaries. They did an excellent job, got attention for their work, and moved up the organization. This is the exception, not the rule, but it can and does happen.

In and of itself, the job can be a lot of fun. Good secretaries take a lot of the responsibility off their bosses' shoulders, handling a lot of business for them. It doesn't have to be a job of typing and filing. It can include managing the administrative staff, handling clients and business associates, screening job applicants, and any number of activities delegated by your boss. If your boss is the assistant equipment manager, it will probably be fairly routine stuff. If your boss is the commissioner of baseball, or chairman of the International Olympic Committee, or owner of the San Francisco 49ers, every day can be exciting and challenging. As responsibility grows, so does the amount of respect you earn. And so does your paycheck. As any executive will tell you, once he or she forms a partnership with a good assistant, that person becomes invaluable. Most executives are willing to pay accordingly.

Getting a job as a sports secretary requires good skills, especially in the area of computer use and word processing. One very important element is to take the job for what it is. If a sports organization thinks you are such a huge fan that you won't be able to do a professional job when a player walks by, you won't get hired. Also, if you think that you will be in that slot for six months and then advance to another position, don't bother applying.

Sports organizations need people in administrative roles, and they like to keep them there a long time. But if you have the skills, honestly want to be a support person, and like sports, you have a chance to get the kind of job you want. It takes persistence. Keep your resume updated and in the hands of the person who hires administrative staff people. Offer to work as a temporary helper when you know he or she has a big project coming up. In sports as in most other professions, if they see you can do the work and they like you, you will eventually get a job.

WHERE THE JOBS ARE: Any and all sporting organizations.

KEYS TO GETTING THE JOB:
• Good basic office skills, especially familiarity with computers.
• Willingness to do the job. If you are "settling" for being a secretary but really want to move into something else within the company fairly quickly, make sure it is understood. Many companies want people who are not motivated to move up the corporate ladder to fill those positions.
• Professional appearance and demeanor.

SECURITY

POSITION: Security

EDUCATION/TRAINING: Training in crowd control, security.

SALARY: Intro: $5–$6 per hour
Average: $20,000
Top level: $100,000

JOB DESCRIPTION: Sporting events put very large numbers of people in relatively small areas. As common sense will tell you, if you have a large number of people in a small area, the potential for problems is pretty high. Stopping these problems before they start, or before a small problem becomes a big one, is the job of the security professional.

Contrary to their image, the main job of security people at a sporting event is not to police the crowd for wrongdoers. The primary concern is just dealing with the large number of fans, moving them in, out, and around facilities safely. Second on the list would be customer service, providing information to fans about the facility, giving directions, and locating such things as bathrooms and concession stands. Third would be handling emergencies, managing evacuation procedures, being familiar with and able to administer CPR, and knowing how to access the emergency medical staff. Then would come the activities we would traditionally assign to security people, things like breaking up fights, removing drunks, and apprehending pickpockets.

Security staffs for sporting events are typically made up of two groups—the security professionals and law enforcement personnel. Teams, facilities, and event promoters will usually make use of both groups, hiring the law enforcement people on a part-time basis from the city, county, or municipality where the event takes place, and having the security people in full- or part-time staff positions.

Sports jobs in security are fairly readily available for the qualified individual. Teams and facilities are constantly trying to upgrade their security staffs. As the amount of different responsibilities for the security person grows, so does the difficulty in finding qualified people. The size of the staffs required to do the job is huge. At a typical baseball game, over 200 security people may be on hand to manage the crowd. Jobs may range from guarding the ticket takers to sitting on the end of the team bench at a basketball game to keep fans away from players.

In addition, many teams and events use outside security firms to provide manpower. These firms have hundreds of individuals on staff and assign them as needed to sporting events, concerts, political rallies, and so on. While hooking up with one of these companies would probably not result in working in sports every day, it would offer great variety and would get you some experience in the field.

WHERE THE JOBS ARE: Arenas, stadiums, teams, leagues, events around the country, no matter how big or small.

KEYS TO GETTING THE JOB:
• Proper license; state requirements fulfilled.
• Clean criminal record.
• Good verbal and written communication skills.
• Experience in military or law enforcement, if possible.

SPEAKER'S BUREAU

POSITION: Speaker's bureau manager

EDUCATION/TRAINING: No specific background required.

SALARY: Intro: $18,000
Average: $25,000
Top level: $50,000

JOB DESCRIPTION: The demand for today's professional athletes and coaches to make public appearances is phenomenal. Everyone wants to hear what they have to say, on almost any issue. On the other side of the equation, top athletes and coaches who are good speakers can supplement their income substantially, sometimes to the tune of hundreds of thousands of dollars. Or they can use their popularity to raise money or awareness for a specific cause they are interested in supporting.

So on one side you have groups from all walks of life clamoring for people to make speeches. On the other, you have sports professionals who want to make some money or give something back to the community. Who helps these two groups get together so that everyone is happy? The speaker's bureau manager.

The speaker's bureau manager can work for a variety of organizations. Teams, facilities, leagues, corporations, magazines, and agencies all have speaker's bureaus. They act as matchmakers, teaming the sports celebrity with the event, negotiating the fee, and handling all of the details. If they work for a particularly popular athlete, the job may be to just screen all the opportunities and give him the top two or three to choose from every month. If they work for a team, the job may be to get as many representatives to as many events as they can, hoping to create more interest in the team. And if they work for a corporation, the job may be to solicit groups they want their representative to speak to, in order to meet some specific business objective.

Essentially, the job is one of networking, scheduling, and attention to detail. You find the interested group, arrange for the speaker to be there on the right day at the right time, make sure all of the contracts and agreements are signed, and solve problems when they arise. In professional sports, speakers usually get more requests than they can handle, so the job also includes letting people down easy, trying to not disappoint them too much. The Twelfth Street Baseball Card Trading Club will never get the free appearance by Nolan Ryan it is after, but its members are still fans and have to be treated professionally, and with respect.

Essentially an administrative position, this career doesn't pay extraordinarily well. But if you enjoy working with athletes and coaches in an "off the field" environment, it is a great job to have.

WHERE THE JOBS ARE: Teams, facilities, leagues, independent speaker's bureaus, corporations, magazines.

KEYS TO GETTING THE JOB:
• Having the trust of the athletes and coaches or someone in the organization.
• Ability to be very diplomatic with people.
• Organization and detail-handling skills.

SPECIAL EVENTS

POSITION: Special events manager

EDUCATION/TRAINING: College degree preferred.

SALARY: Intro: $18,000
Average: $35,000
Top level: $85,000

JOB DESCRIPTION: Special events in sports run the gamut, from events as large and impacting as the Major League Baseball All-Star Game and U.S. Open golf tournament to a small luncheon with a sports theme to kick off a television station sales campaign.

In order to properly plan and coordinate these kinds of events, many teams, facilities, corporations, and agencies have created a position known as special events manager. This job is really made up of a string of special projects. One time it may be the company's involvement in a local golf tournament, the next time planning and executing an annual sales meeting using athletes or coaches as speakers.

Typically, the special events manager has all of the resources and none of the manpower. In other words, you can use anything the company has to get the job done, but the planning, managing, and most of the execution is done by you. Most special events managers have a great deal of autonomy and a lot of exposure to upper management. Planning and making arrangements for a twenty-fifth anniversary celebration can take months. In the end, however, it is the chairman of the board who makes the speech or cuts the ribbon. And if all goes well, the special events manager gets the credit, from the top down.

This is another job for the detail-minded person. It requires good knowledge of your business and the marketplace. A good special events manager is very well connected in the community, with contacts in a wide variety of areas. If your event needs a charity involvement, you better know which charity to call. If you decide to have a parade down Main Street to welcome home the national champions, you have to be able to pick up the phone and get the needed permits and manpower overnight.

Anything and everything outside the day-to-day business routine can qualify as a special event. It is this variety and the constant challenge to do things in unique and entertaining ways that supply a lot of the reward in this job.

Getting a job as a special events manager first requires some background in putting on and managing events. This kind of experience is readily available in college, putting on concerts or intracollegiate sporting competitions. It is also possible to get involved with nonprofit organizations as a volunteer. They will gladly give you as much responsibility as you can handle for their 10K run, celebrity basketball game, or other fund-raising event. Once you have some experience in these areas and have made some contacts in your community, you will be ready to take a full-time position in sports special event management.

WHERE THE JOBS ARE: Facilities, teams, advertising and marketing agencies, corporations involved in sports, leagues, governing bodies, colleges, media outlets.

KEYS TO GETTING THE JOB:
• Good knowledge of the community.
• Ability to problem-solve creatively.
• Good head for details.
• Some event experience.

TELEMARKETING

POSITION: Telemarketer

EDUCATION/TRAINING: No specific requirements.

SALARY: Intro: Hourly
Average: $25,000
Top level: $50,000

JOB DESCRIPTION: The amount of telemarketing—marketing via the telephone—taking place in sports is increasing dramatically. Colleges use telemarketing campaigns to boost contributions to the Athletic Department fund. Professional teams hire telemarketers to boost season and individual-game sales. Media outlets use telemarketers to solicit advertising or to test how their programming is received. In the end, it adds up to a lot of people who get paid to talk about sports on the phone all day.

The job of telemarketing is relatively clear-cut. You spend your day calling prospective buyers, customers, and clients and trying to sell them something or getting information from them in the hope of being able to make adjustments in your program to be able to sell them something in the future.

To be a successful telemarketer takes training and skill. To sell season tickets, for example, you have to be very familiar with the team, with the players, with the facility, with the benefits of owning season tickets, with all of the special promotions taking place, and must be able to overcome the objections of the potential buyer. It takes an infinite amount of patience, and a thick enough skin to not take rejection personally.

In the right program, with the right product, telemarketers can make a very good living. Most telemarketers get paid on a commission or bonus program, with incentives for making more calls and for being successful on a greater percentage of calls and generating more revenue. The bottom line is, if you make money for the company, the company will take care of you.

Many sports entities hire outside telemarketing firms to work on specific projects. These telemarketing firms don't specialize in sports per se, but they may have ongoing relationships with enough sports events and teams that by joining one and making your preferences known, you could find yourself working on sports projects almost full-time.

Getting a job as a telemarketer is relatively easy, if you are willing to work part-time and odd hours. Contact the sports organizations in your area and see what their needs might be in this area.

WHERE THE JOBS ARE: Professional teams, facilities, colleges, telemarketing firms, racetracks, media outlets, research companies.

KEYS TO GETTING THE JOB:
• Good telephone voice.
• Patience.
• Knowledge of the product.
• Ability to take rejection.

TELEVISION

One of the most coveted careers in sports is a career in sports television. Most of the sports events and activities seen by fans today are seen on television. It's where the action is, hopping around the city, the country, or the world covering the most exciting events. Also, because television is such a familiar part of our daily lives, it all looks easy. "Anyone should be able to do it. Why not me?"

In fact, this analysis is partly right. Even in these days of tightening production budgets, there are thousands of jobs in sports television across the country. Nearly all of these are technical in nature, requiring special skills or training in order to get them. Unfortunately, many people have unrealistic expectations of what they can do in television and how quickly they can reach their ultimate goal. If your goal is to start out being a television network broadcaster, you will most likely fail. But, if your goal is to work in sports television, you have some skills, and you are willing to start at the bottom, you will most likely succeed.

Jobs in television production follow a particular pathway. Just about everyone in production starts as a production assistant, doing everything from getting coffee for the staff to producing a short piece on the city in which an event is taking place. Using this position as a training ground, people move up either within their organization or by changing jobs. Each step along the way adds more responsibility and more pressure, until you get to the top positions, which are producer and director. These are the most coveted jobs in television sports, because they control what goes over the air. It is very difficult to enter this job progression anywhere but at the beginning. It is sort of like taking college courses—you must fulfill the prerequisites before you can take the next steps. Please keep this in mind when reading about careers in television.

The following are the categories of jobs available in sports television:

POSITION: Associate director

EDUCATION/TRAINING: Television production experience; good technical background.

SALARY: Intro: $30,000
Average: $50,000
Top level: $75,000

JOB DESCRIPTION: The associate director is not an assistant to the director, as the title may imply. Rather, he has specific technical responsibilities for both taped and live shows.

For taped shows, the AD is the person responsible for taking all of the video "building blocks" available to him in the editing room and putting them together to create a show. Examples of these building blocks may be the raw footage from the event, the opening tease for the show, tape of past events from the tape library, clips from other shows, interviews, highlights, different music beds, and so on. All of these are put together in a certain way to tell the story of the event and to give the show the kind of feel that is interesting and exciting to the viewer.

For live shows, the AD has three main responsibilities. These are: working with the videotape replays, coordinating the production with the studio, and inserting the preproduced taped packages into the broadcast.

During a game, the AD is constantly looking at videotape replay machines. When he finds a replay that is particularly meaningful, he relays that to the producer, who decides whether or not to use it. All of this takes place in split seconds. It takes a thorough knowledge of the game at hand. For example, during a basketball game it is entertaining to show a replay of the tremendous dunk shot Charles Barkley threw down at the end of a play. However, a better replay would be a shot of the entry pass that set up the dunk. This would give the announcers a chance to analyze the play, to comment on why the guard was able to make that pass, and to speculate on how it could be defensed the next time. In short, to the basketball fan the story of the play wasn't the dunk shot, it was the pass. By selecting the right replay, the AD can tell that story.

Production coordination with the studio is a simple but necessary function. During a remote broadcast, the AD is on the phone with someone back at the studio, coordinating the commercial breaks. The AD alerts the studio that a minute-and-a-half break is about to come up. He counts it down, and at the right moment the studio person plays the commercials. When the commercials are about over, the studio counts that down to the AD in the field, who relays it to everyone in the truck. This counting down back and forth by telephone may seem unnecessary, but it insures accurate timing of the breaks, prevents dead airtime, and helps smooth the transition from the broadcast to the commercials and back again.

The last job of the associate director is to manage the insertion of preproduced packages into the broadcast. He has to be familiar with what and where they are, so that they can be called up the instant the producer or the director wants them. For example, before a Chicago-Oakland baseball game Carlton Fisk may be asked ten questions. One of them will be what Chicago's strategy is when Rickey Henderson leads off an inning. During the game, if this situation comes up, the AD would remind the director that they have it on tape, and he may or may not call for it. If he does, the AD has to know exactly where it is and how to call it up in an instant, to insert while Rickey is taking his warm-up swings.

The position of associate director is the training ground for directors, and in some cases producers. The technical expertise and creative experience gained in the job prepare you to move to that next level. It can be a pressure-packed job, but for those who survive and thrive in this position, the next step to director is not far behind.

POSITION: Associate producer

EDUCATION/TRAINING: Television experience, probably as a
broadcast associate.

SALARY: Intro: $25,000
Average: $40,000
Top level: $60,000

JOB DESCRIPTION: The role of the associate producer is less
well defined than that of the associate director. This job typically
deals more with planning the format of a show than with the technical
aspects of putting a show together. The associate producer is in
charge of coordinating the format, or plan, of the show. He makes
sure that all of the pieces of the broadcast are in place and ready
to go.

For example, he sees that the AD has done all of the features for
insertion, that the promotional copy for the talent to read is done,
that the billboards (the sponsors before and after the show) are ready,
and that the show graphics are prepared. Associate producers also
work with the talent, making sure they have the information and
support they need to get the job done. In a sense, it is the job of
being an assistant to the producer, sharing the responsibilities of
planning and organizing the production, as contrasted to an associate
director's job, which is very separate from the director's responsibilities.

POSITION: Audio technician

EDUCATION/TRAINING: Degree in audio engineering; union
membership may be required.

SALARY: Intro: $25,000
Average: $45,000
Top level $100,000 plus

JOB DESCRIPTION: The audio technician is responsible for set-ting up and managing the sounds of sport, from the crack of the bat hitting a baseball to the roar of the crowd. Most of the work done by this group of technicians takes place before an event, making sure microphones are in place and working. During a game, the audio technician makes sure the sound levels are adjusted to correspond with the action of the event while allowing the announcers to be heard.

Most of these positions require specialized training in audio engi-neering. Many require membership in a union. However, there are always some entry-level positions that require nothing more than the strength (and sometimes courage) to pull cable under stadium steps and through tunnels to make the audio connections. By starting in an apprentice program and doing jobs like this, you can have the opportunity to learn on the job and eventually get more responsi-bility.

POSITION: Broadcaster

EDUCATION/TRAINING: Degree in broadcasting or journalism; experience with a particular sport.

SALARY: Intro: $8,000 or less per year, seasonal or part-time
                 Average: $60,000
                 Top level: $1,500,000 and up

JOB DESCRIPTION: The sports broadcaster is the person most closely identified with sports on television. The jobs range from sports reporter on a local station to network host for the Olympic Games. These are the people who tell us about the event. Their personality and insight adds to our enjoyment of the sport, as well as helping us keep track of the action.

On a local level, most broadcasters are reporters and newsreaders who specialize in sports. They go out in the field with a camera and sound crew, tape the stories, and present them daily as part of a regular news format. In addition, they may be involved in broadcasts involving local teams, such as preseason NFL contests or local NBA and Major League Baseball games. Or they may broadcast local events, such as high school football or state championships.

The smaller the city, the more broadcasters have to do on their own. In some small markets, they must act as their own camera, sound, and editing crew. In the largest markets, they may not have to do anything except read the sports every night on the air. As a general rule, though, most broadcasters are responsible for researching the sports and events they are covering, for writing what they are going to say on the air, and for helping to edit the tape that is going to appear on the air.

On the regional or network level, the job is essentially the same. The broadcaster is the person seen on the air, the one who describes the action and helps us understand the sounds and pictures we have seen. The only differences are in the technical aspects of the broadcast, the amount of people involved in the broadcast, the audience, and the salaries. Everything is bigger.

Getting a job as a television broadcaster is one of those things that appears easy on the surface but that, when you look into it a little bit, seems impossible. The truth, of course, is somewhere in the middle. The jobs are tough to come by, but there are openings every year around the country. With more and more regional cable companies getting into sports broadcasting, the job market is about as good as it ever has been in terms of the number of jobs out there.

The place to start a broadcasting career is in school. Many colleges offer courses and even majors in television. With that kind of preparation, the next step is to work. Take any job in any size market you can get, and do the best you can with it. Television broadcasting is one of those professions that has no real on-the-job training program. You just have to do it. Later, as you get more proficient and develop your style, you will have the opportunity to change jobs, to move to a slightly larger market or a bigger station. Most television sports announcers have changed jobs a half-dozen times or more to get where they are now. It is a tough road, with little security, but if you have talent you will succeed.

POSITION: Broadcast associate

EDUCATION/TRAINING: College degree in broadcasting, journalism, liberal arts.

SALARY: Intro: $25,000
Average: $28,000
Top level: $30,000

JOB DESCRIPTION: The position of broadcast associate, sometimes known as production assistant, is the entry-level position in television sports. The responsibilities of the job can vary widely. At the Super Bowl, a BA for the network might be a glorified gofer, in charge of making sure the announcers get to the airport on time. A few months later, for a major golf tournament, he or she may research and produce a special segment on what the golfers do on their day off.

At local television stations, these are the people who do things like tape baseball games, marking the times when key plays occurred to ease editing later. It is a typical entry-level position, including lots of busywork, tedious tasks, and, on the flip side, many opportunities to learn what goes into a sports telecast.

Most of the producers and directors in television today started their careers as broadcast associates. It is a great way to get on-the-job training and make some money (though not a lot) at the same time. The typical associate starts with a station or network as an intern while still in school, then moves into a job after graduation. It is very competitive, especially on the network level, but at least it is a proven system with a direct pathway to the jobs of producer and director.

POSITION: Camera operator

EDUCATION/TRAINING: Technical school degree, college degree preferred; union membership often required.

SALARY: Intro: $35,000
Average: $60,000
Top level: $100,000

JOB DESCRIPTION: Camera operators at sporting events are directly responsible for the pictures we see on television. Whether stationed high above the press box for a football game or running from sideline to sideline shooting a basketball game with a Minicam, it is the view of the camera operator that we see on our screens at home. The excitement, the drama, and the humor of sports are only as entertaining as the images they find to focus upon. The announcer may tell us how proud a kid's parents must be of their daughter. But a picture of mom's smiling face, with a tear in her eye, says it much better.

First and foremost, it is the job of the camera operator to capture the action of a sporting event; to make sure the viewer sees what happens, clearly and completely. Beyond that, the best ones also try to find pictures that help us feel like we are there and that convey the essence of what is happening.

Camera operation is one of the most physical of television jobs. If you are a camera operator at a stock car race, you will have to carry your camera from one end of pit row to the other, often in very hot weather. Fixed-position end zone cameramen who work in open football stadiums during snowstorms will tell you that you can get awfully cold standing in one place for four hours. But being a camera operator means you will be in the thick of the action all day long—which is a very exciting place to be.

As with most technical jobs in television, camera operators start their careers in school, learning how to operate the equipment. They then move to small-market stations, learning how to shoot all kinds of events, including sports. They may get a free-lance job now and then when the networks come into their area for a special event.

They change jobs to go to work for a network affiliate, giving them a chance to do more and more sports. After a couple of more moves and some more years of experience shooting sports for the local station and the networks, they could eventually find themselves in a position to be hired by a network, where they get the chance to shoot a Super Bowl or a World Series.

POSITION: Chyron/electronic graphics operator

EDUCATION/TRAINING: Technical expertise.

SALARY: Intro: $25,000
Average: $50,000
Top level: $80,000

JOB DESCRIPTION: Electronic graphics machines, called Chyrons, are computers that act as very sophisticated typesetters. Sitting at a console and typing in a series of codes, the operator can produce letters, numbers, logos, and other graphics in a wide variety of colors, shapes, and sizes for the television screen. While on the surface this may seem to be a small part of television, it is actually crucial to the broadcast of sports.

Everything on a television screen except the raw pictures from the camera is produced and run through the Chyron. The score of the game, information about the athletes, the starting lineup, notes on an upcoming telecast, current standings, promotional announcements— the list goes on and on. Next time you watch a sporting event, count the number of different times you see words or graphics on the screen. The number may surprise you. And it underlines the fact that the Chyron operator is one of the busiest members of the team during a telecast.

Most of the Chyron operator's work is done before the telecast. The basic framework for all the different graphics to be broadcast is laid down and numbered. That way, during the telecast when the director calls for the starting lineup, the operator can call it up at the push of a button. Sports being what it is, new information must be created on the run. If the director wants stats on what a baseball player has done in his previous three at bats, the framework can be called up, the numbers can be filled in, and it can be ready in seconds.

The job runs the gamut, from the tedium of putting in information days in advance to the tension of creating the graphic to illustrate the point your announcer is making on the air RIGHT NOW. The Chyron operator's knowledge of the event and ability to plan for a variety of situations can make the difference between a satisfactory broadcast and a great one.

POSITION: Director

EDUCATION/TRAINING: College degree in broadcasting, journalism, or liberal arts; member of Directors Guild.

SALARY: Intro: $25,000
Average: $50,000
Top level: $750,000

JOB DESCRIPTION: Sports television directors are responsible for everything you see on your screen when you are watching the event. Sitting in a television studio or mobile unit, the director manages the broadcast. Looking at a wall of television monitors showing all the shots of all the cameramen, the director decides which ones go on the air in which order. He decides which graphics get up, when to go to commercial, which replays to use.

If a game is exciting, the job is easy. If it is a blowout, the director's job is to work with all the elements at hand to keep the viewers interested.

Directors are the artists of sports television, responsible for making a game an event, an athlete a star. The best ones are the most valuable employees behind the camera in sports television, and are compensated as such. With that responsibility comes a lot of pressure to perform. Since much of sports television is live, the director is constantly faced with the challenges of cameras breaking down, key replays being lost, and all of the human errors that become magnified when they are witnessed by thousands or millions of people. All of these situations must be taken in stride and worked around to produce the best telecast possible. It is an intense job, one of the most powerful in sports television, and definitely not for the fainthearted.

One of the top directors in the business today is Joe Aceti of CBS Sports. Joe has directed all of the big sporting events, from the World Series to the Olympic Games, in a career that has spanned thirty years. He started in television right out of college, as a production assistant at ABC. He gradually moved up the production ladder to assistant director, then to director on some minor shows, and finally got to direct a major sporting event. The process, from college graduate to director, took over a dozen years. Even with all of the changes in television since he started in the early sixties, the path followed by Joe Aceti is still the best way to build a career as a network television director.

If your goal is to direct local television, you should target your job search toward small-market television stations or cable systems that produce local programming. While the pathway is similar to that at the networks, the time schedule may be greatly accelerated in these situations, allowing you the chance to direct sooner. Once you have produced a body of work you can show, you can start looking for opportunities in larger markets.

POSITION: Engineer

EDUCATION/TRAINING: Degree in engineering; certification; union membership often required.

SALARY: Intro: $25,000
Average: $45,000
Top level: $60,000

JOB DESCRIPTION: Delivering a television picture and sound to your home involves a tremendous amount of often temperamental technical equipment. Add to this the challenge of broadcasting live events from remote locations, in weather ranging from freezing to broiling. And to that add the yearly (if not monthly) new electronic breakthrough that requires additional training to operate and repair. It is easy to see how important the contributions of the people who maintain, repair, and often manufacture this equipment—the engineers—are to sports television.

The term "engineer" here refers to the technical people who make sure all of the equipment in the studio or in the field is set up and ready for the broadcast. They are the ultimate behind-the-scenes people, whose work is noticed only when something goes wrong. They're the offensive linemen of television.

The job of engineer includes a wide variety of activities and levels of expertise. The introductory level includes such tasks as running cable from trucks to broadcast locations, often under stands and in other areas where people were not meant to go. It includes keeping the equipment maintained and troubleshooting on the spot when breakdowns occur. It may include working with satellite uplinks and downlinks, making sure the signal gets where it is supposed to go. Often it means making split-second decisions on the run, with only your experience and the tools you have in your pocket available to solve a problem.

Every television station, cable company, mobile broadcast company, and television network has a very large engineering department. People need to be on hand twenty-four hours a day seven days a week, in case problems arise. While turnover is low, the sheer number of available jobs means that opportunities do arise in this category fairly regularly. One thing to be aware of is that many of these positions require membership in a labor union.

Getting a job as a broadcast engineer requires a strong educational background. In many cases, especially for jobs in upper management, a college degree is required. Many schools around the country offer courses in broadcast engineering. This is the best place to start pursuing your career in this field.

POSITION: Floor director/stage manager

EDUCATION/TRAINING: College degree in broadcasting,
                     journalism, liberal arts.

SALARY: Intro: $25,000
                   Average: $40,000
                   Top level: $100,000

JOB DESCRIPTION: The position of floor director or stage manager in sports television is a mid-level production position. The floor director works with the announcers in the studio or at an event. He is the person who lets them know when they need to go to a commercial, tells them how long they have before they are back on the air ("We're on in three, two, one . . ."), works with them on reading promotional copy, tells them when to go to special features, even makes sure they are dressed properly for an on-air appearance.

The floor director helps the announcers maintain the flow of the broadcast, while at the same time insuring that all the elements are included at the right time. He is in direct communication via headset with the director at all times, receiving instructions and relaying information to the talent.

The job of floor director is a step up from the position of broadcast associate, but is still a fairly junior position on the production team. While students just out of school shouldn't hope for a floor director position as an entry-level job at a network or a major market station, it is possible in small markets to do some floor directing fairly quickly, especially if you have done an internship at the station or if you have gotten some good free-lance experience.

TELEVISION • 255

POSITION: Producer

EDUCATION/TRAINING: College degree in broadcasting, journalism, liberal arts.

SALARY: Intro: $25,000
Average: $50,000
Top level: $500,000 and up

JOB DESCRIPTION: The producer is the person in charge of the television show before and during the telecast. The decisions made by the producer make the difference between a mediocre and a terrific sports broadcast.

The producer is the one who structures the show. He lays down the framework everyone will work from, from the opening billboards to the end of the broadcast. It is the producer who hires the staff. He selects the director, the announcers, the technical staff, the camera and audio people—everyone needed to put the show together. He decides what the show will look and feel like, then guides the on-air talent and the director toward that goal. He also creates and develops story lines, the main themes of the broadcast.

For example, he may decide that a key to a football game will be how well the Redskins handle the Philadelphia pass rush. The announcers will be prepared to discuss the subject, and the director and camera crew will be looking for shots that reflect that story line.

In short, the producer is the general manager of the broadcast. All of the planning and all of the preparation are his responsibility. The success or failure of any particular broadcast depends on the producer and the team he has assembled.

During the broadcast, the producer sits next to the director, working with him to get the kind of a show he wants. Often, the producer picks the replays to be used. And he may be in direct contact with the on-air talent, providing information on what to expect from graphics or replays. During the broadcast the director calls the shots—he is in charge of what goes over the air. But since the end result is the responsibility of the producer, he has a lot of input during the broadcast.

Producers and directors often work in teams. This builds a relationship between them and results in a consistency from broadcast to broadcast. The same producer and director do every game of Monday Night Football, for example. In today's cost-conscious times, the titles are often combined into one position, the producer-director. The producer-director not only plans the broadcast, but directs it as well.

Because the ultimate success or failure of a sports broadcast rests with the producer, the position can be very stressful. It can also be very rewarding, both financially and professionally. It is, after all, the producers who go on stage and pick up the Emmy awards every year.

Becoming a producer is a long process, taking you through many phases of a broadcast operation. Because a producer has to assemble a team to broadcast an event, he has to be very knowledgeable about what every member of that team can and cannot do. It is therefore crucial that he spend time working with audio technicians to learn that side of the business, with graphics people to find out what they can do, with camera people and talent, and on and on. Gathering this kind of experience takes time, but it is the only way to become an effective producer.

POSITION: Statistics/research

EDUCATION/TRAINING: College degree in liberal arts.

SALARY: Intro: $15,000
                  Average: $25,000
                  Top level: $35,000

JOB DESCRIPTION: Sports today is dominated by statistics. The numbers of sport come at us from a variety of sources, from baseball guidebooks to sports bureaus that do nothing but handle and analyze statistics. Earned run averages, hang times, plus/minus ratios, first-serve percentages—the list goes on and on. Television makes great use of these facts and figures, so much so that they have created staff positions to research and manage statistical information.

A television researcher/statistician investigates the past performance of athletes and teams, trying to find trends, tendencies, or just tidbits of information that will make the broadcast more interesting. Like archeology, this work entails spending a lot of time going over past histories to unearth some nugget of information. It can be tedious, but it is also a creative endeavor, challenging the researcher to notice things no one has discovered before about an athlete's performance in a given situation.

During broadcasts, the statistician is even more important, especially during football broadcasts. After each play, figures are updated on yardage, carries, passes, tackles, and all the other statistics you hear during the broadcast. This information is an important part of the broadcast. Fans want to know if a quarterback is 6–16 or 15–16, or if a running back is closing in on a hundred-yard rushing day. And if an athlete is approaching a record, his statistics may be the key story line of the game.

Some more job details: the statistician works beside or behind the broadcasters, depending on the amount of room and the configuration of the press box. Some announcers have their own personal statistician, who travels with them for every broadcast. Or a station or network may have a pool of researchers who work on different events as they come up. In many cases, a team or event will provide a statistician or stats crew for all the broadcasts from the team's home stadium or arena.

A good way to break into this field is to work part-time on one of these stats crews. These positions are usually paid per event. For example, for each college football game broadcast you work in your town, you may receive $50. It isn't a living, but it is a great way to get familiar with the business. Your local college or professional teams will sometimes have openings for people in this area. If you let them know you are interested and they have an opening, you will get a chance to see what the field is like.

POSITION: Technical director

EDUCATION/TRAINING: College degree in broadcasting, engineering, liberal arts.

SALARY: Intro: $25,000
                   Average: $40,000
                   Top level: $100,000

JOB DESCRIPTION: The technical director is one of the key individuals in any sports broadcast, behind only the producer and director in importance to the success of the show. The technical director is the person responsible for carrying out the director's orders, for actually doing the switching from one shot to another, putting in the fades, wipes, Chyron graphics, and effects you see on television. He is also the supervisor of the technical staff, including the camera and sound people, engineers, video-replay technicians, and Chyron operators. The producer makes the plans, the director calls the shots; it is up to the technical director to deliver the sights and sounds.

During a broadcast, the technical director sits beside the producer and director, in front of a large console. This console, filled with switches and dials, puts all of the technical equipment and effects at the TD's fingertips. As the director calls out instructions, the technical director executes them by throwing the switches and moving the dials and levers. When the director and technical director are in sync, they can anticipate each other's thoughts, resulting in a smooth, flowing broadcast.

A few years ago, technical directors were affiliated with either a television network or a station. More and more, especially in sports, broadcasts are being produced using regional mobile broadcast facilities, such as Northwest Mobile Television. These companies provide the equipment for remote broadcasts, and they are also able to provide much of the staff, including the technical director. Coupled with the rise of regional cable systems, technical directors are now able to make a substantial living by being independent contractors. Wherever the mobile unit goes, wherever there is a sports broadcast, they hire on to switch the show. It is an arrangement that can be very lucrative for the person willing to travel and who can work with a wide variety of producers and directors.

Getting a job as a technical director, as with most jobs in television, requires experience. This is not a position anyone will be able to just step into. But by getting a good educational background and concentrating on the technical side of the business, you should be able to progress to this level within a few years.

POSITION: Unit manager

EDUCATION/TRAINING: College degree in business, liberal arts.

SALARY: Intro: $25,000
                    Average: $45,000
                    Top level: $125,000

JOB DESCRIPTION: The unit manager on a sports television production is perhaps better characterized as the business manager. The unit manager is accountant, personnel director, travel agent, and technical manager.

Included in the unit manager's responsibilities are insuring that all of the equipment arrives at the remote broadcast site, on time and in good working order; making all necessary travel arrangements for staff; hiring part-time staff members; arranging telephone lines and satellite feeds; doing advance work, such as broadcast site selection; monitoring hours and working with union representatives to insure that everyone gets breaks on time and that overtime is kept to a minimum; distributing per diem and salary checks; writing checks to cover all the incidental expenses of the production at the remote location; and distributing and collecting the proper tax forms and documentation from all of the workers on the job. It is a job that requires a large degree of patience, strong organizational skills, and the ability to work with people under pressure.

Jobs as unit managers usually go to people with strong human resource, accounting, and budget management skills. This is one of the least technical jobs in television, having more to do with managing people than working with equipment. It still requires expertise in the area of production, however, which means it falls along that producer/director career pathway.

POSITION: Videotape operator

EDUCATION/TRAINING: College degree in liberal arts.

SALARY: Intro: $18,000
                 Average: $30,000
                 Top level: $75,000

JOB DESCRIPTION: The videotape operator manages the television replays, so important in today's sports telecast. From the studio or the remote broadcast facility, the videotape operator monitors the action of the game from his unique vantage point. If the replay he has shows more about a play, is clearer, is more exciting, or is perhaps just different, he lets the producer and director know and they call for it.

At the largest events, such as the Super Bowl and the World Series, the production staff will include a half-dozen or more videotape operators, each looking for that unique camera shot that shows whether the receiver was out of bounds, or if the ball was fair, or the tremendous break on that putt on the 17th green.

WHERE THE JOBS ARE: Television jobs are located where the television stations, networks, cable companies, regional sports networks, and mobile production facilities are located: major metropolitan areas. The larger the market, like New York and Los Angeles, the more opportunities exist. Many part-time jobs in television exist at the site of onetime events, such as golf tournaments. In general, to move your career forward in television you have to be willing to move where the jobs are.

KEYS TO GETTING THE JOB:

• A college degree. Though television is a relatively young industry, most people entering the field today have a strong educational background.

• Technical skills. As described, many of the jobs in television are technical in nature. If you have experience in electrical engineering or electronics, or with the equipment used in television, you are a step ahead.

• Willingness to travel. This includes moving from market to market to gain experience, as well as working at remote broadcast locations, sometimes for months at a time.

• Willingness to do what it takes. Most of the people in sports television today started "at the bottom." That means hauling electrical cable in the snow. That means doing play-by-play of high school baseball. That means getting coffee for announcers. That means a student internship for no pay. The goal is to become one of the television family, to learn, and, when you get an opportunity to show your stuff, to go for it.

• Union membership. Many of the jobs in television require membership in a labor union, such as the IBEW, AFTRA, IATSE, and the Directors Guild. Check to see which union has the labor contract in your area of interest.

TICKETS

POSITION: Ticket operations

EDUCATION/TRAINING: College degree in liberal arts.

SALARY: Intro: $15,000
Average: $25,000
Top level: $100,000

JOB DESCRIPTION: Ticket operations is the actual handling of tickets, from printing to distribution to collection. Any event that requires a ticket for admission also requires people in ticket operations.

Ticket operations staff members work for teams, facilities, colleges, promoters, and independent ticket services like Ticket Master and Ticketron.

Jobs in ticket operations have evolved greatly over the past ten years or so, with the advent of computer systems. Computer-generated tickets have replaced most of the old hard stock tickets in sports. In this system, tickets are only printed as they are needed. This is not only much more efficient, it is more secure. Since unused tickets are like money, having them preprinted and in storage was something of a security risk.

Typical jobs in ticket operations include working with computer software systems to set prices for maximum revenue generation; printing and distributing tickets to selling locations; doing customer service; handling season tickets; managing will-call areas and working with the ticket sales and collection staff; plus all of the jobs in accounting for tickets that are part of any major operation.

Ticket operations is a very good way to get into an organization. The jobs are relatively low paying, but turnover is somewhat high and jobs are available on a regular basis. The reasons for turnover are many, including the somewhat monotonous nature of the job after you have mastered it and the high level of customer interaction involved, most of which deals with handling complaints. It is nevertheless one of the few areas at a facility, team setting, major college, or event that will accept people willing to work hard with no experience at all.

WHERE THE JOBS ARE: Ticket services, facilities, teams, events, organizations, anywhere tickets are sold.

KEYS TO GETTING THE JOB:
• College education preferred.
• Attentiveness to detail.
• Clean security record.

POSITION: Ticket sales

EDUCATION/TRAINING: No specific background required; college degree in sports administration preferred.

SALARY: Intro: $22,000
Average: $35,000
Top level: $100,000

JOB DESCRIPTION: Ask ten sports marketers how they started in the business and six of them will tell you they started selling tickets. Ticket sales are the lifeblood of sports. There are professional sporting events because people buy tickets to them. College football and basketball have grown into huge profit centers because, first and foremost, people buy tickets to see the games. When sports franchises move, the reason given is often that they didn't sell enough tickets.

Ticket sales jobs are easy to describe. You are in charge of the sale of tickets to the public. This requires the usual steps in making a sale, such as finding prospects, qualifying those prospects, making your presentation, and closing. No different from selling a lot of things, really, except for one ingredient. That ingredient is emotion.

People get caught up in sports. They would sooner sell their firstborn child than their priority seats to the Indy 500. Nebraska Cornhusker season tickets are the topic of custody battles in divorce courts. In many people's eyes, having Super Bowl tickets between the 40's says "success." The people in sports ticket sales have learned how to use that emotional attachment to make a sale.

Sports ticket sales jobs break down into three areas. These are season-ticket sales, group-ticket sales, and individual-ticket sales.

In season-ticket sales, the packages you are selling include every game of the season. These clients are either the most enthusiastic fans around or businesspeople who use the tickets to entertain their customers and employees. Season tickets are expensive. Even though they are typically discounted, it is still a large cash outlay for the buyer. The disposable income of the average season-ticket holder is, naturally, higher than the average fan's.

Season-ticket sales take place for the most part in the off-season. Some of the business is call-in or referral, but most of it is a result of good, solid prospecting and cold calling.

Season-ticket sales are the backbone of a sports franchise. They mean that there is guaranteed attendance every night. They also mean money in the bank, in advance, which teams, facilities, and promoters can then put to other uses. Because they are so important, usually the best, most capable salespeople are in season-ticket sales.

The next important sports ticket sales job is in group sales. You've heard the announcement and seen it on the readerboard a dozen times: "The Cowboys welcome the following groups to today's game: the Fort Worth Boys Club, Dallas Ladies Auxiliary Number 239, and the Downtown Baptist Church Senior Men's Choir." These groups of twenty or more make up a substantial part of ticket sales. They are of great benefit because the groups themselves act as ticket salespeople, rounding up enough people to get over the minimum required. And they can be directed to specific, predetermined events, such as a Little League Day in baseball when all of the Little Leagues in the area are invited, swelling attendance figures and generating a lot of excitement, perhaps enough that they will decide to come back on a later date individually.

Group sales, like season-ticket sales, require solid prospecting and cold calling to put together. They also require some organizing and hand-holding, to make sure groups round up enough people, get their money in on time, and get their special requests taken care of. Those in group sales, like those in season tickets, are usually some of the better salespeople. Group sales also take place in the off-season, but unlike season-ticket sales continue all through the year.

The final group is the individual-ticket salesperson. This is the person who actually stands at the facility and sells tickets to the public or answers call-ins for credit charge calls. These are entry-level positions but give you valuable experience in answering questions and handling the public. Some individual tickets are sold just prior to the opening of the event or season, but for the most part they are sold during the season.

Compensation in ticket sales is usually a combination of salary and commission. Most experienced salespeople would rather work on commission, since it gives them the chance to maximize their income based on their own performance. Sales in sports can be cyclical—if a team wins the Stanley Cup, sales the next year will be brisk. But if it fails to make the playoffs, things can be a lot tougher.

As mentioned, ticket sales are a good way to get into a sports organization and show what you can do. Many a successful sports executive earned his or her first recognition by selling tickets. If you give it a chance, and are willing to start at the bottom, it can work for you.

WHERE THE JOBS ARE: Major sports franchises, organizations, promoters, ticket agencies, facilities.

KEYS TO GETTING THE JOB:

• Good organizational skills.
• Ability to sell.
• Thick enough skin to take some rejection and come back and try again.
• Professional appearance.

TRAINER

POSITION: Trainer

EDUCATION/TRAINING: Degree in life science or physical therapy; master's degree preferred. Certification by NATA; license from by the state you wish to practice in, in most states.

SALARY: Intro: $20,000
Average: $35,000
Top level: $100,000 plus (with bonus)

JOB DESCRIPTION: The job of athletic trainer has gained a tremendous amount of importance in sports over the past ten years. Today's athlete is paid an enormous amount of money to perform. It is the job of the trainer to enable him to do so. This is accomplished by helping the athlete prevent injury, by keeping minor injuries from cutting down playing time or hindering performance, and by working with the medical staff to speed recovery from major injuries and surgeries.

The trainer covers the middle ground between two groups, well athletes and sick athletes. Well athletes on the professional level and in many colleges get help preparing themselves to compete from strength and conditioning coaches. Sick or injured athletes are attended to by the medical staff. The trainer communicates with these other professionals and manages the day-to-day treatment of the athletes. In cases where a conditioning specialist is not on hand, the trainer takes over that role.

The level of education, the techniques, and the kinds of equipment involved in being a professional team trainer have advanced tremendously in the past two decades. Putting on ice or sitting in a whirlpool have been replaced by using ultrasound, electrical muscle stimulation and computerized isokinetic exercise machines. A thorough knowledge of kinesiology and biomechanics is now not a luxury, but a requirement to keep up with the many changes taking place every year in the field.

Athletic trainers are required to obtain certification from their national governing body, the National Athletic Trainers Association. This involves passing an oral exam, a practical exam, and a written exam. In addition, many states now require the practitioner to have a license from the state, which includes both a written and practical exam. The state licensing concept is expanding, and will probably be law in every state before too long. In addition, trainers have to take continuing education classes every year in order to maintain their certification by the NATA.

The job of team trainer includes a lot of one-on-one contact with the athletes. Each injury and each person is different, and the trainer must devise a different program for each one. A good trainer must also be part psychologist, since a patient's mental attitude is such an important part of the recovery and rehabilitation process.

The number of people on a training staff can vary a great deal. A typical collegiate staff will have a head trainer, perhaps a second head trainer for women, several assistant staff trainers, a couple of graduate assistants (who are still in graduate school but receive some money for their work), and a group of student assistants. A large program may include twenty or thirty student assistants. A professional staff will be much smaller, with a head trainer and a couple of assistant trainers.

Because of the ever-increasing interest in sports and the large number of participants in sports at all levels, a tremendous need exists for athletic trainers. With the proper educational background, you can virtually be assured of a job in training once you are certified and licensed. You will not start out as head trainer for the New Orleans Saints. But, you will have a lot of opportunities to work with athletes on some level, and after you gain some practical experience, who knows?

WHERE THE JOBS ARE: Professional teams, colleges, sports medicine clinics.

KEYS TO GETTING THE JOB:
• Solid educational background; master's degree preferred.
• Experience in sports medicine. Get it by volunteering on the high school level, or doing student internships, or working in a clinic part-time.
• NATA certification; state licensing, if required.

TRAVELING SECRETARY

POSITION: Traveling secretary

EDUCATION/TRAINING: No specific requirements; college
degree preferred.

SALARY: Intro: $25,000
Average: $35,000
Top level: $100,000 plus (with bonus)

JOB DESCRIPTION: The job of traveling secretary is specific to
baseball. It is the person who handles all of the travel, transportation,
and housing needs of the team on the road, from spring training to
the World Series.

The job includes working with airlines, charter companies, and
hotels to negotiate the best rates and most effective routes for team
travel. The traveling secretary also works with the stadium operations
people to make sure baggage and equipment get where they are
supposed to. In short, they are the exclusive travel agents for the
players and coaches. Many a ball game has avoided postponement
through the creative efforts of the traveling secretary and his ability
to get a team into and out of a city anytime, in any weather.

The typical traveling secretary also acts as a sort of administrative
staff person on the road for the players, giving them restaurant and
entertainment suggestions, organizing activities for off days, helping
them with ticket requests, and in general looking out for them and
their families on the road. It is this more personal, unwritten part of
their job that makes traveling secretaries part of the team, and it is
why when it comes time to vote playoff and World Series shares,
they are often included.

Most traveling secretaries working today started in other jobs with
a baseball team. These jobs include working as an assistant public

relations director, or in the scouting department, or in some other front office position. They had some success, got exposure to the baseball side of the job (as opposed to the business side), and then moved to the traveling secretary spot when it opened.

WHERE THE JOBS ARE: Major league and some minor league baseball cities.

KEYS TO GETTING THE JOB:
• Travel industry background.
• Ability to work with players.
• Organizational skills, attention to detail.

VIDEO COORDINATOR

POSITION: Video coordinator

EDUCATION/TRAINING: Training in operation of video
equipment.

SALARY: Intro: $20,000
Average: $30,000
Top level: $50,000

JOB DESCRIPTION: Many professional sports teams now have
their own video coordinator on staff as a permanent employee. The
video coordinator has nothing to do with the broadcast of games or
events. Rather, his area is scouting and player development.

The video coordinator tapes every practice and every game. This
tape is then broken down for study, to determine what a team's
tendencies are, to identify strengths and weaknesses, and to monitor
individual performances. Opposing team tape is also broken down
for study, to try to unscramble opposing offensive and defensive
strategies and to evaluate personnel.

For instance, a hockey coach may look at the last twenty examples
of the opposing team on the power play. From this, he may get the
information he needs to kill a key penalty in the next game against
that team.

Because of the relative ease of videotaping compared with filming,
plus the wide variety of editing possibilities that exist with tape, the
videotape coordinator is constantly busy. One day he may be doing
a practice, another working on prospects for the upcoming draft. In
today's world of technology in sports, the use of videotape has been
one of the most important breakthroughs in the past decade.

The job itself requires a good deal of training or technical background, especially in the area of editing. Plus, you only get one

chance to shoot a game, so it has to be done correctly. But once the techniques have been learned, the execution of the job is fairly routine.

Getting a job as video coordinator usually begins in college, working with your athletic department. After you have gained experience in the area, you will be a step ahead when you enter the job market.

WHERE THE JOBS ARE: NFL teams, some NBA, NHL, and Major League Baseball teams.

KEYS TO GETTING THE JOB:
• Technical expertise in videotaping and editing.
• Thorough knowledge of the sport.

LEAGUE INTERNSHIP PROGRAMS

You can write or call these organizations for information about their internship programs.

Major League Baseball
350 Park Avenue
17th Floor
New York, NY 10022
(212) 339-7800

National Basketball Association
645 Fifth Avenue
10th Floor
New York, NY 10022
(212) 826-7000

National Football League
410 Park Avenue
14th Floor
New York, NY 10022
(212) 758-1500

National Hockey League
650 Fifth Avenue
33rd Floor
New York, NY 10019
(212) 398-1100

National Hot Rod Association
2035 Financial Way
1st Floor
Glendora, CA 91740
(818) 914-4761

Index